Prophecy
Its Reality and Use

Paul Akimoto

**A Rainbow in the Clouds
Publishers**

Xulon
PRESS

Published by A Rainbow in the Clouds Publishers
3-22-11-501 Hongo, Bunkyou-ku, Tokyo, JAPAN
Web Site : http://www.kumoniji.co.jp/

Copyright© 1999 by A Rainbow in the Clouds Publishers
Translation copyright © 2013 by A Rainbow in the Clouds Publishers

Cover photo by Minoru Kitano
Cover design by Samuel Kasahara Nobuo

www.xulonpress.com

Contents

CHAPTER 1

Prophecy should be eagerly sought after

Many Christians frown upon the word "prophecy." This may be because they sense something fanatic about this word, or because it sounds far removed from the true Christian objectives of personal sanctification and missions. Or, it may bring to mind past problems that prophecy has caused in some churches. Given all that, we cannot really blame those Christians who believe that prophecy is something dangerous, extreme or false and something to keep away from. But, is this the true nature of prophecy? Should prophecy be treated as something dangerous, something to be shunned like a savage, wild dog? Of course not. The Bible tells us of the importance of prophecy.

In this short book, referring to the Bible and to my own experiences, I would like to discuss the true nature of prophecy, its wonderful blessing, how to use it, the danger of misusing it and the importance of examining it.

"Prophecy" or "prophetia" in Greek means receiving God's words in trust and telling the words to others, or talking in place of God. It includes fore-telling, but not that alone. It means receiving in trust all of God's words including His teachings, His instruc-tions, His love, His judgments, His promises, etc.

In the New Testament, prophecy is sometimes used to mean a sermon (e.g. Romans 12:6), and some other times to mean prophecy as the gift of the Holy Spirit (e.g.ICorinthians Chap.14). In this book, I am going to deal with the latter, i.e., prophecy as the gift of the Holy Spirit.

My definition of the gift of prophecy is "the words that are given to a Christian by the Holy Spirit and are spoken directly through that person." Since those words are from God, they will be spoken within the framework of the Old and New Testaments, which are the complete revelation given by God. They will never go out of that framework; there can be no new revelation.

My introduction to prophecy

It was sometime in 1975, when I heard words of prophecy for the first time in my life. At that time, while I belonged to an evangelical church, I received a blessing of the gifts of the Holy Spirit. Together with some other members with the same spiritual experi-ences, we started a small prayer meeting group. The leader of the group who advised us was a lady, who had the gift of prophecy, and joined our prayer meeting several times, although she was living in a distant city in the western part of Japan. Every time words of prophecy were spoken out in the deep presence of the Lord, I was moved and I felt with all my heart: "The Lord is alive."

Those days were my infant period in terms of the growth of spiritual gifts. I knew that the Bible spoke about prophecy, but didn't learn about it enough, with only a limited knowledge of it. I was just an excited onlooker and felt as if I were living in a dream.

A little while later, the Lord led me out of that church over the issue of the spiritual gifts. I went to a church where the spiritual gifts had begun to occur even though it was of the evangelical stream. In that church the gift of prophecy was not working yet, but a prophetic word was spoken out one night in the prayer meeting we held privately on Sunday nights. It was spoken out by one of my juniors of the seminary.

At that time I was deeply discouraged because I was going through an extremely difficult trial. But a prophetic word was told, saying "You will be protected to the end." The moment I heard those words, I became quite skeptical because I thought that the person who prophesied might have spoken out his own idea. But next moment, another prophecy was told, which drastically changed my view. It said, "The difficulty you are now facing is much easier to overcome than the one that is to come later in your life." This prophecy really touched my spirit. The discouragement in my heart disappeared, and I felt strength rising up within. I felt through the strong witness of the Holy Spirit that the Lord had certainly spoken. Those words were enough to restore me. The Lord further said to me, "Ask questions and I will answer you." I was astonished to hear that, but thought: "If I ask questions aloud, the person prophesying may listen to me, and answer himself. So, I had better ask a question in my mind silently."

In my mind I asked God a question. To my surprise, immediately after I asked it, the proper answer came to me through the person who was prophesying. Never before, have I experienced anything like this. Surely the Lord was alive and spoke. The experience of asking a question and getting it answered happened just once that time, but it strongly remained in my heart.

The Lord told me further through prophecy that I would later visit various places for His ministry. Now, I go throughout Japan from Okinawa to Hokkaido and many countries throughout the world. In January 1996 I ministered in India; in February, the U.S.; in April, the Philippines; in May, Brazil; in June, the U.S. again; and in July, the former Yugoslavia.

Certainly, what God speaks will come true. I have learned and witnessed the wonderful blessing of prophecy. But at the same time, I have experienced problems with prophecy.

Incorrect Prophecy

When I moved away from my home church, I joined a local charismatic church because it was convenient for me to attend as a seminary student visited the church only on special occasions like retreats. The members of the church were very committed and self-sacrificing.

However, they started to go to extremes, such as "By reading books about faith other than the Bible, Christians will be spoiled by human wisdoms." One day, I heard them insisting that Christians were not saved unless they spoke in tongues. I then realized that there was a problem in that church. We are saved if we believe in Jesus Christ. Salvation has nothing to do with speaking in tongues.

A while later, in obedience to what God was showing me, I wrote a letter requesting permission to leave the church. Then, I got a reply back, saying, "Come to the church immediately. It is a matter of your salvation." So, I went to the church with one of my friends, and was requested to join a prayer meeting. Soon, many words of prophecy began to be spoken out. They said, "Stay in this church," "Satan is working in you" and "You will be in big trouble if you leave this church." However, I had anticipated that such prophecies would be told about me at the church. So I had prayed, "If you would talk to me, God, please do so not using prophecies. Otherwise, I cannot tell whether You are telling me or people are speaking out their ideas."

Obviously those prophecies were wrong. In obedience to God I left the church and was greatly blessed as I followed His path. The members of that church were all wonderful people, but the prophecies they spoke then were from their own thoughts.

In the area of prophecy I have seen: God's overwhelming power, human mistakes and errors, and Satan's misleading power. These experiences have become a starting point of my full-scale involvement in prophecy.

Biblical Use of Prophecy

About twenty years have passed since I experienced what I described in the previous section. Since that time, I have heard of various prophecies. Some revealed wonderful manifestations of God's work and glory, but some others turned out to be foolish human mistakes or, even worse, sometimes resulted in very tragic errors.

Therefore, prophecy, an excellent gift and weapon from God seems to have been kept away from by Christians. The idea that prophecy is dangerous has been held not only in the Evangelical stream, but even in the Pentecostal and Charismatic streams.

Beware of falling into the error of experientialism! We cannot judge prophecy only by looking at the results of incorrectly used prophecy. When prophecy is used biblically, it is totally effective in achieving its purpose. Criticism against prophecy and mistakes in the use of prophecy by those who believe in it, seem to come from the same root of not using it the way the Bible tells us to.

One day, an excellent machine was installed in the church office. It was a great help at first, but then it suddenly stopped working. Nobody could get it to work again; it was left unused for half a year and it soon became covered with dust. I became very suspicious of the manufacturer and felt that we were unfortunate to have bought such defected machine. Since I could not leave it like that forever, one day I asked a machinery expert to check it. He looked under the table on which the machine was placed and had the machine working again as before in less than a few minutes. Can you guess how he did it? He just plugged it in. The machine was out of use for half a year because it wasn't plugged in. Neither the machine nor the manufacturer was at fault. The cause of the problem was simply that the machine was not being used properly, and it was an elementary mistake.

Problems with prophecy, in many cases, apparently stem from the wrong use of prophecy. In other words, it is not being used in accordance with the Bible. So, although it is an excellent spiritual gift from the Lord, prophecy can cause some problems.

The machine in our church office has been working normally since it was plugged in. It has not been broken down at all, for it has been used properly. This rule applies to prophecy as well. The Bible never says, "Don't seek prophecy because it will bring problems," or "You may neglect prophecy as it is not necessary."

First of all, plug into the power source of faith and use prophecy in the right way.

God's work in our church through Prophecy

Our church was established in April, 1984 at Kokubunji City, Tokyo. At the beginning, regular attendants of the church services were around fifteen people. Six months later, the work of prophecy started in our church.

As of May 1996, our daughter churches, from Okinawa to Hokkaido, number forty-five. About 370 students, from all over Japan, are learning in our seminary. Our missionary work overseas has extended into many countries in Asia, Africa, Europe and North and South America. Daughter churches have been established in the Philippines, Los Angeles, and London. Missionaries have been sent to New York and Israel.

In all of these works, prophecy played a very important role. Actually, prophecy has an important role in doing God's works. Not using prophecy is just like we fight with an enemy only with swords instead of guns. We should use prophecy, an indispensable weapon for the spiritual breakthrough in Japan, and for the coming, great, end-time harvest. We should learn the Bible well so that we can use prophecy in accordance with the Bible. When we use it biblically, not depending on our experiences, prophecy will become a great power.

Prophecy in the Bible

Let us read the verses in Chapter 2 of Acts that quote Joel's prophecy:-

'And it shall come to pass in the last days, says God,
That I will pour out of My Spirit on all flesh;
Your sons and your daughters shall prophesy,
Your young men shall see visions,
Your old men shall dream dreams.
And on My menservants and on My maidservants
I will pour out My Spirit in those days;
And they shall prophesy.
I will show wonders in heaven above
And signs in the earth beneath:
Blood and fire and vapor of smoke.

The sun shall be turned into darkness,
And the moon into blood,
Before the coming of the great and awesome day of
the Lord.
And it shall come to pass
That whoever calls on the name of the Lord shall be
saved.' (Acts2:17-21)

This is the prophecy fulfilled on the day of
Pentecost; Peter and the other disciples received the
Holy Spirit, were filled with the Holy Spirit and began
speaking in tongues. The last days began from this
very day, and so did the days of the Holy Spirit. If
we carefully read this prophecy, we can see that it is
only partially fulfilled and the rest is yet to come. This
is because there was no blood, no fire and no rising
smoke on the day of Pentecost. The sun has not turned
into darkness and the moon has not turned into blood.
These have not yet been fulfilled. The phrase, "the great
and awesome day of the Lord", which follows these
unfulfilled prophecies, refers to the Second Coming of
Christ. From this we can see that this prophecy foretold the Second Coming of Christ as well as Pentecost.

The Bible goes on to say, "Your sons and your
daughters shall prophesy, Your young men shall see
visions, Your old men shall dream dreams." Many
of the visions Ezekiel saw were prophecies. Some of
Daniel's dreams were prophecies. The Bible sums up
all of these with the word "prophesy", saying, "And
on My menservants and on My maidservants I will
pour out My Spirit in those days; And they shall
prophesy." Interestingly enough, Joel talks about two

15

things concerning the last days: the pouring out of the Holy Spirit and prophecy.

From the Bible, I believe that before the Second Coming of Christ, the Holy Spirit will be poured out and prophecy will be used. I also believe that as God gave Israelite the former rain and the latter rain, so He gave us the former rain on the day of Pentecost and will give us the latter rain immediately before the Second Coming. Through the former rain, He poured out His Spirit on people and gave them the Holy Spirit. Through the latter rain, He will pour out His Spirit on us and bring about the Revival on earth, the final and great harvest.

Prophecy as a spiritual gift

Now, brothers and sisters please stop and think. Why did Joel speak about prophecy, but not healing, miracles, or speaking tongues? Why not about faith, discernment of spirits, the word of wisdom, the word of knowledge or the interpretation of tongues? This is because prophecy has a position of special importance in the end times.

The First Corinthians 14:1 says, "Pursue love, and desire spiritual gifts, but especially that you may prophesy." Read it carefully. It demands that we pursue not only love, but both love and spiritual gifts.

I have heard many people putting forward various opinions. For example, "It is love that we should strive for, not spiritual gifts," "If you seek spiritual gifts, you will be off the track," and "Wasn't the church in Corinth confused over the gifts of spirit issue?" However, read the Bible carefully. Paul wrote to the church in Thessalonica which was free from such problems, "Do not quench the Spirit. Do not despise prophecies." (1 Thess. 5:19 and 20)

Trying to adapt the Bible to someone's opinion will create contradiction. This is because an opinion is not biblical truth but only a person's idea. The Bible clearly tells us that we should pursue both love and spiritual gifts. It does not tell us to eagerly pursue healing, miracles, or tongues, but to eagerly pursue prophecy.

"Prophecy" certainly holds a special position among the spiritual gifts. The Bible talks about prophecy in such a way that it takes precedence over the other gifts. Why is this so? It is because this spiritual gift holds an important key to the work and will of God.

Chapter 2

God's work through
directive prophecy

❧

Mission to Brazil

We went on a mission trip to Brazil for ten days from May 21, 1996 as a part of overseas mission works from our "The Water Flowing from the Sanctuary Mission."

For many years we had been receiving God's directions to start mission work in Brazil. He specifically spoke about setting up of a church, opening of a mission office and sending a long-term missionary. In particular, around two years before that mission trip, a prophecy was told which said that a vessel of the Lord for this mission was already prepared in the suburbs of São Paulo.

However, in spite of those words from God, we didn't have a clue to start ministries in Brazil. Establishing a church and a mission office there, and sending a long-term missionary were more of a dream than a reality.

In the first half of 1996, prophecies about mission work in Brazil began to be given again. They said that a way would be opened to mission work in that country, and that a church and a mission office would also be established there. There were prophecies also for sister M who had previously had a word from the Lord to go to Brazil as a long-term missionary. The prophecies instructed her to hurry with her preparations, such as learning Portuguese, for the time to move to Brazil was near.

However, how could our church go ahead with the work in Brazil? It had no means to do so. I examined the prophecies and confirmed that they were from God. I then decided to take a step of faith even though there was no possible way in sight.

At that time a Japanese Brazilian man, who married a lady member of our church in February 1996, started coming to our church every Sunday. I asked him to contact churches in Brazil. Later, I learned that he had connections with many churches in that country.

This contact opened up a way to nation-wide ministry in Brazil: two radio stations, a church of the Holiness stream for Japanese Brazilians, a suburban church in São Paulo, a church of 2000 members in Brasilia, and a Presbyterian church in Manaus on the Amazon. To my surprise, the churches in Brasilia and Manaus were well known throughout the country. I have been involved in overseas mission work for about ten years, but I have rarely seen such an incredible way of opening up ministry.

Just before leaving Japan for Brazil, a prophecy

given at an all-night prayer meeting said that a church would be started in the suburbs of São Paulo.

After we arrived in Brazil, a miracle happened. A visa was promised to sister M, who had been told by the Lord to be a long-term missionary to Brazil. She decided to stay in the country without returning to Japan, because her visa was to be issued several months later.

(Note: The visa was eventually issued much later than initially told, because the Aum-cult incident took place around that time. As a result stricter laws were made regarding visas for religion-related immigrants. That change prevented her from obtaining the visa for some time. After that time of trial she obtained a two-year visa in October 1998. Now, while waiting for a permanent-resident visa, she was ministering at a church in Rio de Janeiro.)

There was one more miracle in store. When we ministered in Itapebi, a couple kindly took care of us. Their eldest son, a seminary graduate was a preacher and he had an evangelistic radio ministry which broadcasted to one million people. He lived in a town called Jandira in suburban São Paulo. When he heard our vision to establish a church and mission office in Brazil, he sensed God's prompting, and offered to take charge of both works. I confirmed God's will immediately when he made that offer, and decided to accept it.

Before leaving for Brazil, we had no clue and no idea as to how we could promote mission works in that country. However, when we were about to return home from Brazil, a long-term missionary was already stationed in that country. Both a church and a mission office were to be set up in Jandira in suburban São Paulo (about one hour by train from the city center). Now, as the prophecy predicted, a church and a mission office are operated in suburban São Paulo, and as the prophecy said, sister M works in that country as a missionary. God accomplished this plan of His, which surpassed our thoughts and hopes by far.

Various functions of prophecy

God speaks to people in various ways, for example, through the Bible; in prayers; by visions and dreams; by a ministry of the Holy Spirit; by His direct voice; through our circumstances; by other people; through prophecy and in many other ways. Among these, prophecy is one of the most important ways God uses to speak to His people.

God teaches through prophecy:

"But he who prophesies speaks edification and exhortation and comfort to men." (1 Corinthians 14:3) Prophecy edifies, exhorts and comforts.

Furthermore:

"But if all prophesy, and an unbeliever or an uninformed person comes in, he is convinced by all, he is convicted by all. And thus the secrets of his heart are revealed; and so, falling down on his face, he will worship God and report that God is truly among you." (1 Corinthians 14:24-25)

As is written above, God reveals Himself to unbelievers through prophecy.

Also, the Book of Acts says:

"Then one of them, named Agabus, stood up and

showed by the Spirit that there was going to be a great famine throughout all the world, which also happened in the days of Claudius Caesar." (Acts 11: 28)

This verse shows that, through prophecy, God gives people prior notices and warnings about the future, and that He gives directions to people.

Directive Prophecy

One of the functions of prophecy is to reveal the plans of God and to give directions. This function is highly important, but somewhat confusing as well. Of course, the problem is not with prophecy itself, which is a gift from God, but with the way people use it. The Bible says, "Let two or three prophets speak, and let the others judge." (1 Corinthians 14:29) As this verse says, prophecy must be examined. People should obey prophecy only after it has been confirmed that it is from God. Also, when directive prophecy is given, its receiving end needs to adopt a certain attitude. That is, the person's heart must be committed to obeying the voice of God. Without an attitude of obeying the voice of God, the hearer would just be confused.

Examples of directive Prophecy

Chapter 42 in the book of Jeremiah describes the scene of Johanan, the son of Kareah, Jezaniah, the son of Hoshaiah, and others asking Jeremiah to seek for God's guidance on their behalf.

"Please, let our petition be acceptable to you, and pray for us to the Lord your God, for all this remnant (since we are left but a few of many, as you can see), that the Lord your God may show us the way in which we should walk and the thing we should do." (Jeremiah 42:2-3)

When Babylon destroyed Judah, those who were not captured and taken to Babylon were under the control of Gedaliah, the son of Ahikam the governor However, since Gedaliah was killed by Ishmael, a man from Judah, Johanan, Jezaniah and others were afraid of retaliation by Babylon and asked Jeremiah the prophet whether they should flee to Egypt or stay in the area under Babylon's control.

Jeremiah said to them, "I have heard. Indeed, I will pray to the Lord your God according to your words, and it shall be, that whatever the Lord answers you, I will declare it to you. I will keep nothing back from you." (Jeremiah 42:4)

Jeremiah asked God for direction about what Johanan and Jezaniah should do. Ten days later, the word of the Lord, prophecy came to Jeremiah:

"If you will still remain in this land, then I will build you and not pull you down, and I will plant you and not pluck you up."..... "If you wholly set your faces to enter Egypt, and go to dwell there, then it shall be that the sword which you feared shall overtake you there in the land of Egypt; the famine of which you were afraid shall follow close after you there in Egypt; and there you shall die." (Jeremiah 42:10, 15 and 16)

God told the people of Judah, who were left alive, not to go into Egypt. Jeremiah said to them as well, "The Lord has said concerning you, O remnant of Judah, 'Do not go to Egypt!' Know certainly that I have admonished you this day." (Jeremiah 42:19).

However, after all, the people left in Judah did not obey God and they came to a tragic end. I wish they had obeyed the Lord.

In the Old Testament days, God actively used prophecy to give directions to His people. David is a good example of a person to whom God spoke through prophecy.

There are similar examples in the New Testament: "Now in the church that was at Antioch there were certain prophets and teachers: Barnabas, Simeon who was called Niger, Lucius of Cyrene, Manaen who had been brought up with Herod the tetrarch, and Saul. As they ministered to the Lord and fasted, the Holy Spirit said, 'Now separate to Me Barnabas and Saul for the work to which I have called them.' Then, having fasted and prayed, and laid hands on them, they sent them away." (Acts 13:1-3)

The words spoken by the Holy Spirit in the above passage are prophecy. People of the church in Antioch, in obedience to the directions given by God, set apart Barnabas and Saul for the work they were called to, and sent them away.

Directive Prophecy and listening to and obeying God

Directive prophecy is of great importance in doing God's work. Why is it so? Of course the functions of edification, exhortation and comfort are also important, but the function of directive prophecy is different from other functions. Giving or receiving directions is closely related to the fulfilling of God's plans. God has a great plan for this generation. We should implement that plan by following God's directions. We should listen to and obey God.

However, there are two alternative ways in following God: One is to guess what you think God wants, and the other is to ask God for directions and obey them. These two ways vary greatly in effectiveness. A guess can often be wrong. On the other hand, asking God for directions is the foundation for fulfilling His will correctly. We should not be mistaken about the things that we are called to do.

About one month after I dedicated my life to the Lord, doctors found out that there was something wrong with me. After that, I vomited blood many times. I was hospitalized for a time and then had to make regular visits to the hospital. This lasted for five years, which really upset me. I asked God many times why it was only I who had to suffer for so long, because I felt I was being judged by God.

However, when I asked the Lord, He told me that He was training me how to dedicate my life to Him. The Lord impressed upon me to read the life stories of George Mueller, Hudson Taylor, Oswald Smith and others who were all trained through illness. I then understood that it was training for me, and learned a lot of lessons in that situation. That learning experience established in me a strong foundation for devoting my life to God.

Guessing sometimes causes misunderstanding. In human relationships we see tragedies caused by guessing. However, when we ask God, we can find out things correctly. Asking God and listening to Him is a major point in faithfully implementing the Lord's plans.

Establishing churches and Prophecy

In August 1994 God told me through a prophecy to plant a church in Sendai City. I examined the prophecy and got convinced that it was from the Lord. However, I was very perplexed because I knew nothing about the city, had no acquaintances there, and had no idea how to start it.

When I was at home worrying about how to do it, a telephone call came to our overseas mission office from Sendai City. The telephone call was, to my surprise, a request for us to establish a seminary or a church in that city. A person, who had been conducting a regular prayer meeting, had been praying for the establishment of a church there. I didn't know anything about that at all. The person later told me that she had tried to call the mission office several months before for the same purpose, but at that time the Holy Spirit stopped her. However, she was told by the Holy Spirit to telephone the mission office on the same morning I was trying to work out how to get started with a church in Sendai. The Holy Spirit timed it perfectly. The church really started in Sendai City just as the Lord had told me. I was worrying over what to do with it, but the Lord Himself had prepared everything for it.

One day in July 1992, the Lord told me through a prophecy that a church would start in Kyoto City.

At that time, we had small meeting groups in nearby areas, Osaka and Hyogo, but, not in Kyoto. We had no connection there, either. I wondered what to do, but the Lord repeatedly said, "A church will start in Kyoto." Just after that, a meeting was held at our daughter church in Osaka and I delivered a message there, where I met some new attendants from Kyoto. During the prayer time in the meeting, one of our pastors hosting the meeting introduced me to the leader of the people from Kyoto and asked me to pray with him. I felt at a loss for what to pray about, but I agreed and prayed together.

Then, all of a sudden, he eagerly began to ask me to start a church in Kyoto. He told me that there was a group of people with a place prepared for holding a worship service. Until this day, that was the only time I had been ever asked to start a church in Kyoto.

The board of elders confirmed, through prayer, that this was from God and a daughter church started in Kyoto at the end of August, 1992. We learned later that the prayer meeting leader renovated the third floor of his house to a small chapel for worship services and had been praying for a church to start. The church started one week after the renovation was completed although this was not scheduled intentionally. God's works are perfect, and we can only be surprised when we witness them.

God has a plan for each and every one of us, and each and every one of His churches. His plan is marvelous and wonderful, far beyond our thoughts and desires. His plan is fully revealed when we give up our own plans and obey His voice. God shows us His wisdom and power when we obey Him. We will see great things happen and find ourselves in remarkable events.

Prophecy is a mighty power for those who listen to and obey God, because He uses prophecy as an important means to talk to His people. Listening to God and obeying Him changes our lives and our ministries. Prophecy is an important factor in bringing about these changes.

CHAPTER 3

Prophecy is a
God-given weapon

How we started seeking Prophecy

Through God's leading, we started a church in Kokubunji, Tokyo in April 1984. God told us right from the start to live by the principle of hearing and obeying Him. So, we began our work by committing ourselves totally to praying, hearing and obeying Him. Day by day, my fellow worker and I asked God what to do as we prayed and read the Bible. However, it took a long time to receive even one instruction from God. After some time, we earnestly began to desire that we should receive God's instructions more quickly and clearly. We then started to pray eagerly for that.

Around September, one of the church members came to me and said, "Words of prophecy keep coming to my mind during the worship service. May I speak them out?" Honestly speaking, I was very much perplexed at her words. I had been observing the work of prophecy for about ten years so I knew that prophecy had caused many problems. Also, I was concerned about how other people would speak of us if I allowed prophecy to be spoken in the service, for prophecy was in bad repute. However, when I prayed, I felt strongly that the Lord was leading all of this. Finally, feeling as if I were crossing the Rubicon, we decided to allow prophecy to be spoken in the service.

About twelve years have passed since then. Certainly, we have been misunderstood many times and we have gone through difficulties because of prophecy. However, these things are trivial matters compared to the blessings we have received through prophecy: We have been able to experience that the Lord is alive and to take part in His wonderful plans.

The power of spiritual gifts

I was once serving as an assistant pastor at a church. An evangelist of the church was leading a small prayer meeting on Sunday nights. Prophecies were spoken at the meeting. That evangelist invited me, saying, "Words of prophecy are spoken in this meeting. Would you like to join?" I declined his offer at that time, because I thought: "God speaks to us through the Bible and prayer. I don't need to hear Him speak through prophecy." I know now how little I understood about prophecy. God has provided the gift of prophecy for a reason.

If you walk from Kokubunji City to Shinjuku, it takes you well over seven hours (I once did it), while you can travel the same distance in 30 minutes by using a train. If somebody says, "I don't take a train. I walk." I wouldn't oppose that. However, by the time he or she walks to Shinjuku, I could get to Okinawa or to Hokkaido via Haneda Airport, or to Seoul, Korea via Narita Airport. Using spiritual gifts can be compared to this illustration. We can evangelize and edify churches without using prophecy or other spiritual gifts. However, if we use spiritual gifts, we will see the Lord do even greater works. An army can fight a battle only using swords, but it will be much more powerful with cannons and guns.

In Acts 1:8 it says, "But you shall receive power when the Holy Spirit has come upon you; and you shall be witnesses to Me in Jerusalem, and in all Judea and Samaria, and to the end of the earth." On the day of Pentecost this prophecy was fulfilled. The disciples were given the Holy Spirit and received power. Please read this verse carefully here. What kind of power is this? Clearly, it is the power of the Holy Spirit. Then, how was this power of the Holy Spirit manifested? The answer is also clear. It was manifested as the power to be witnesses, and as the power working through spiritual gifts. Spiritual gifts are the weapons that God has provided for expanding the kingdom of God.

My introduction to directive Prophecy

During my seminary student days, I attended the church where I ministered later as an associate pastor. I was also introduced to directive prophecy at that church. While I was still a seminary student, a charismatic holy meeting was going to be held in Hakone

31

(a small resort town located around 80 miles from Tokyo).

I intended to go to that meeting with one of my friends from the seminary in Tokyo. However, we had an argument on Tuesday, two days before the charismatic meeting. He insisted that we leave Tokyo around nine o'clock in the morning because the meeting was to begin in the afternoon. I argued that we should leave around noon, after the morning seminary classes. I thought that it could not be helped if we were late for the first session of the meeting. However, he adamantly insisted on leaving around 9:00 a.m. When it seemed impossible to come to an agreement through discussion, he proposed that we pray to God and ask Him. I thought it was ridiculous to ask God for such a thing, but agreed to pray with him anyway. He prayed, "Please tell us which is better, to leave Tokyo at 9:00 a.m. or at noon to attend the holy meeting in Hakone." But I forgot about that soon.

The following day, I joined a regular prayer meeting at seven in the evening. At the meeting we usually prayed in several groups and I prayed in a group of church workers that evening. While praying, we were so blessed, and I had never experienced such prayer meeting that was so anointed by the Holy Spirit as that evening meeting. The prayers were so strongly led into deeper prayers that we could not stop praying, even when the prayer meeting was over. As it got late, people in the other groups left the meeting. Finally, I was left alone with the church worker. Suddenly, he began prophesying and said, "Leave at 9 o'clock." Of course, I had not talked to him about the prayer I prayed the previous day at the seminary. Far from telling him about it, I had completely forgotten about it myself. He prophesied repeatedly: "Leave at 9 o'clock." Somewhat confused, he finally started praying between the prophecies: "Lord, tell me what you mean by 'Leave at 9 o'clock'." Since I clearly knew what it meant, I immediately explained to him what had taken place on the previous day. Of course, my friend and I left at 9 o'clock the next day. We received wonderful blessings, including healing, in that charismatic meeting.

God speaks and gives directions

In I Kings the Bible tells about King Ahab of Israel, who fought the Arameans. Suddenly a prophet approached Ahab king of Israel, saying:

"Thus says the LORD: 'Have you seen all this great multitude? Behold, I will deliver it into your hand today, and you shall know that I am the LORD.'" So Ahab said, "By whom?" And he said, "Thus says the LORD: 'By the young leaders of the provinces.'" Then he said, "Who will set the battle in order?" And he answered, "You." (I Kings 20: 13 -14)

When Ahab asked, the Lord gave him directions through a prophet. Ahab won an overwhelming victory by obeying His directions. God speaks to us, and if we open our hearts to Him, He gives us directions.

There are many people who do not accept and practice prophecy, and yet still receive directions from God. In a Keswick Convention I heard a Korean preacher give a testimony of his dedication, saying,

"I heard God's silent voice." I have heard many pastors and lay believers give their testimonies, saying, "I was given directions through the Word, in a prayer, or through other people." The Lord speaks, foretells, and gives directions. But prophecy, in particular, is a powerful means that God has provided for speaking, foretelling and giving directions to us.

The direction and work of our church began to change greatly when we started to heed, through prophecy, God's teaching, indications, encouragement, comfort, foretelling, directions, etc. Since our church was founded on the principle of hearing and obeying God, we placed great importance on God's guidance from the beginning. After prophecy was introduced, the works of our church began to be more powerful with more specific instructions.

Faith is the key to opening God's work

Some of you might say, "I cannot believe such a thing." In the past, neither could I. I was saved in an evangelical church but I had quite a liberal belief mindset at that time. I believed in the cross but did not believe in miracles. I did not believe that prayer worked or that Satan existed. I tried hard to figure out what the parable of the Lord feeding 5000 people represented.

My attitude, however, was drastically changed when I read the life stories of George Mueller and Hudson Taylor. Faith began to rise in my heart when I read in the stories how prayers were so marvelously answered and how wonderfully God guided them.

Faith is the key to opening God's work.

For example, the cross of Jesus Christ redeems all of mankind from sin. This is a historical fact, but people cannot receive forgiveness for their sins unless they believe. In the same way, you will not see God's work unless you believe. Chapter 9 in the Gospel of Matthew tells of a woman who had been suffering from a hemorrhage for twelve years. She thought, "'If only I may touch His garment, I shall be made well.'" (Verse 21) "But Jesus turned around, and when He saw her He said, 'Be of good cheer, daughter; your faith has made you well.' And the woman was made well from that hour."(Verse 22)

In this verse, Jesus told her that her faith had made her well. Of course, what made her well was not faith, but God. Faith can be compared to a pipe which God's power passes through. Even though God's power is available, nothing happens without faith. Therefore, when Jesus said that her faith had made her well, He spoke the truth. Without faith, even touching His garment would not have healed the hemorrhage she had been suffering from for twelve years. When she touched Jesus, she was healed of her sickness because she had faith.

The same thing happened to me. When I did not believe, my prayers were not answered; I did not experience either miracles or healings; God did not talk to me, or give me directions. However, when I believed in prayer, my prayer began to be answered. When I believed in healing, I began to experience healings. When I believed in God's guidance, He started giving me directions.

God's work will start when we simply believe what the Bible says. Faith is the key to opening God's work. When you begin to believe in prophecy, you will begin to see His wonderful work through prophecy.

Cooperative relationship with Pastor Merlin Carothers

Pastor Merlin Carothers is the world famous as the author of "Prison to Praise". One day, a prophecy was given, foretelling that he would come to our church. At that time he had never been to Japan, and we did not even know where he lived.

The Lord had repeatedly told us the same thing over several years. Then one day, we had an unexpected telephone call, which said, "Pastor Merlin Carothers is coming to Japan, but it has not yet been decided where he will minister on Sunday in Tokyo. Would you like him to minister at your church on that day?" I was so surprised to hear that because I never imagined it. The Lord did exactly what He had told us He would do.

Later on, the Lord told us that we would form a cooperative relationship with Pastor Merlin Carothers. He went on to say that we would translate and publish his book, "Prison to Praise", in various countries, and that he would be a lecturer in our seminary. Following God's directions, we began to go ahead with those things.

In 1995, we published 2000 copies of Pastor Carothers' book in Vietnamese and in 1996, another 2000 copies in Cambodian. Now underway is translation into Myanmar and into Terugu, one of the languages spoken in India.

Our seminary gives Pastor Carothers' class by tape recording. In February 1996, at the end of the semester, the students who enrolled in his class and I visited him in the U. S. to attend his lecture in person. The Lord opened up the way for the plan that He had told us about.

In July 1996, we released the Japanese version of the video tape, "Prison to Praise". For this release the Lord performed a miracle for us.

When we visited Pastor Carothers in February, we saw the video of "Prison to Praise," which had just been completed in English. Pastor Carothers said, "You can release it in Japan if you like." That made an impression on my heart even though he did not ask me directly to do so. However, when I tried to put that into action back in Japan, I did not have any success. The video tape needed to be dubbed or superimposed in Japanese. I didn't know anybody working in the video industry, and using a production company could be very expensive. We prayed earnestly to God for help.

One day in April that year, a lady asked me the way to the Commerce and Industry Hall when I was on my way to that building for the second Monday worship service. I immediately told her the way, thinking that she might possibly be going to attend the service. She then said, "I recognize your voice. You are Pastor Akimoto, aren't you?" On our way to the building I found that she was in the video business.

On the recommendation of a person who knew her, I asked her to estimate the expenses necessary to make a Japanese version of the video tape. At this point, I did not know exactly who or what she was. Two days later she contacted me, asking me to let her produce the Japanese version. Later, I learned that she was sister S, President of a company called Filmic Vineyard, a company importing educational films from United States and distributing them in Japan. Also, she had been helped through Pastor Carothers' book when she was in difficulty. Furthermore, she offered to pay the cost of producing 500 copies of the Japanese version. She just wanted to do something for God, because her company had been blessed by God since it was established 10 years before. The Lord had prepared for us the person most suited for video production.

God intends to do great things through prophecy. When we use prophecy, we will see His wonderful work and glory. God never gave us the gift of prophecy without a reason. We should take up this God-given weapon.

CHAPTER 4

Everybody can prophesy

❧

Interpretation of the First Corinthians, Chapter 13

Today we live in the age of the Holy Spirit. The Holy Spirit has been powerfully advancing His work since the day of Pentecost, 2000 years ago. The work of spiritual gifts, which was dramatically evident in the time of the Early Church has become evident again. This phenomenon indicates that we are entering a highly important period, like that of the Early Church.

Recently, there have been many arguments about the pros and cons of the gifts of the Holy Spirit. Let us read some scriptures From the First Corinthians, Chapter 13

"Love never fails. But whether there are prophecies, they will fail; whether there are tongues, they will cease; whether there is knowledge, it will vanish away. (Verse 8)"

"But when that which is perfect has come, then that which is in part will be done away." (Verse 10)

Referring to these scriptures, some people insist

that tongues and prophecies have ceased. But, if we read these scriptures carefully, we will see that this is not what they are saying. The scriptures say that love is eternal, but that prophecy, tongues and knowledge have a time limit and will cease and be done away with. The scriptures also set a time, saying "when the perfect comes". Now what does it mean, "When the perfect comes"? Of course, it means the Second Coming of Christ. Therefore, tongues, prophecy and knowledge will last until the perfect comes or until the Second Coming of Christ.

Therefore, the First Corinthians 13:8 and 10 do not say that prophecy and tongues have already ceased as some people think. Rather, these verses say that they will last until the Second Coming. God will use prophecy, tongues and knowledge until the Second Coming.

The chapter goes on saying, "For we know in part and we prophesy in part." (Verse 9) We tend to think that knowledge is almighty, but what we, human, can know is only in part. However, knowledge, though only a part, plays an important role. If Christianity does away with knowledge, it will collapse. In the same vein the chapter says, "we prophesy in part". Prophecy is also partial and not all powerful. However, it plays an important role just as knowledge does. We should not make light of the work of prophecy.

The door is opened to overseas missions

When we were told through prophecy that we would be involved in overseas mission work, I could not take it seriously.

When I was a student, a message about missions in Indonesia delivered by Rev. Okuyama inspired me to dedicate my life to God as a missionary. However, years passed by and the way wasn't opened to a missionary so I forgot about it. At that time my mind was fully occupied with building up a church in Kokubunji City in Tokyo.

But the Lord showed me His plan for Japan, and, through prophecy, His plans for overseas missions. Without prophecy, we would not have become involved in the overseas mission work we have accomplished. When we were told about overseas missions, there was only one person in our church who had a passport. Almost none of the members had been on an overseas trip, and basically they had no interest in going abroad at all. As for me, I had never even traveled by airplane.

Besides, most of us, including myself, could not even speak English, which was considered the minimum requirement for overseas missions. We did not know how to go about it; we did not have any support or any connections through which to start the work. But the Lord, through prophecy, directed us in the area of overseas missions. We examined the prophecies and confirmed that they came from God. We started praying about overseas missions.

God's word is different from that of man. It always comes true. Some people said that our overseas mission work would never happen and some thought it was ridiculous. They thought so because they looked at us instead of God's words for us. We were dropouts, most unsuitable material for overseas missions, but it was God who had spoken the words. For several years we just prayed. Many times I thought that it would not work, but through prophecy, the Lord encouraged us and kept on saying to us, "I will send you throughout the world."

Then, one day, the Lord directed us, through prophecy, to send a team to Nagasaki. The Lord told us to pray in preparation for an overseas mission trip which would be sent out immediately after it. He also told us that this trip to Nagasaki was to give us training, as the overseas mission outreaches would be carried out in teams. I was only half convinced, but obeyed what the prophecy said because we had confirmed that it was from the Lord. Eventually, five teams went to Nagasaki. Immediately after this, the door to overseas mission work was opened for us, starting with the smuggling of Bibles to China.

As the Lord told us, our overseas mission work was done in the form of teams. So far, nearly one hundred outreach teams have been sent out from our mission. We have ministered in all of the continents of the world, except Australia. As of 1996 we have daughter churches in Los Angeles, London and in the Philippines, and we are starting one in Brazil in September, 1996. We are preparing to start one in India. Eight long-term missionaries (not including voluntary lay helpers) have been sent out into various parts of the world. The Lord has plans for us. And His plans will be fulfilled. We should not make light of the words that the Lord has spoken to us.

Earnestly pursue Prophecy

The First Corinthians 14:1 says, "Pursue love, and desire spiritual gifts, but especially that you may prophesy." Interestingly, it tells us that we should pursue love, and then says that we should desire spiritual gifts.

Here and there I have heard the opinion that states, "Because love is important we should pursue love, not spiritual gifts." I have also heard some others, although admitting spiritual gifts, insist that spiritual gifts are not to be pursued as they are spontaneously given.

The Scripture tells us to pursue love, which is of course most important. But it says neither "Pursue love only" nor "Pursue spiritual gifts only." It says, "Pursue both love and spiritual gifts." Of course, love is most important, and everything is centered on it. As Chapter 13, Verse 13 says, "And now abide faith, hope, love, these three; but the greatest of these is love." Acknowledging this, the Bible then recommends that we pursue spiritual gifts. If we seek to live according to the Bible, which is God's inerrant Word, we should pursue spiritual gifts as well as love.

Among the spiritual gifts, God especially tells us to pursue prophecy eagerly. God is not telling us to shun prophecy and not to use it because it is dangerous. He is telling us to pursue it in particular. Therefore, we should eagerly pursue spiritual gifts, especially prophecy. When we obey God, we receive blessing; when we obey Him, we see His work manifested.

"You prophesy"

For several years after prophecy began to be spoken in our church, I was committed to playing the role of an examiner of prophecy. God often told me to prophesy when in prayer or through the Word, but I never felt like doing it.

In June 1988, we went on a mission trip to the Philippines after a couple of outreach teams had been already sent there. The nights were cool and there was a lot of rain while we were there and, as a result, I caught a cold and so did some of the other team members. It was not serious enough to go and see a doctor, but I did not get healed even though I prayed. I was constantly coughing even after coming back to Japan. In July I went on a mission trip to the U.S. and Mexico. During that trip I also kept coughing. On August 2, my second son Benjamin was born, and I hurried back to Japan from the U.S., while still coughing.

Benjamin was born prematurely, and had to stay in the hospital for a while.

I became impatient, because it would be a big problem if I was still coughing when Benjamin came home. He would come out of a germ-free hospital environment into a place filled with germs from a bad cough. I took medicine and prayed, but nothing worked. For the life of me, I could not get the coughing to stop. In fact, I felt that it was getting worse although it was summer time.

To tell the truth, I knew God was speaking to me through this situation. He was saying to me, "You prophesy." I was vaguely aware that God allowed that cough to persist because of my disobedience. However, that idea seemed to me a little absurd and I was still reluctant to try to prophesy, so I still didn't obey Him. The cough persisted as the day drew near for my prematurely born son to come home from the hospital.

One day before Benjamin left the hospital, I thought that I had no other choice and I finally made up my mind to prophesy. I prophesied as earnestly as possible. When I finished, I found that I was not coughing. I thought it would start again soon, but it didn't. I did not know whether it happened when I was prophesying or when I finished doing it, but I was instantly healed. I was then deeply convinced that the Lord really wanted me to prophesy.

This was my personal experience, but the Bible clearly shows that the Lord wants us to prophesy. It is not a sin not to prophesy, but we will miss out on the blessings the Lord wants to give us through prophecy if we do not obey Him. The words of scripture: "but especially that you may prophesy" are not empty words.

All can prophesy

Once you take up prophecy, you will notice one scripture: "For you can all prophesy one by one, that all may learn and all may be encouraged." (1 Corinthians 14: 31) This Scripture says, "you can all prophesy". "All" means everyone, that is, every Christian.

A servant of God from the U.S. said, "I would like all of you to prophesy." Hearing that, I felt that he was being extreme to say such a thing. However, the Bible definitely says that "all" of us can prophesy; this is the word of the Bible.

But here, some people may point out what the Bible says in Chapter 12 of the First Corinthians contradicts that. It says, "to another the working of miracles, to another prophecy, to another discerning of spirits, to another different kinds of tongues, to another the interpretation of tongues. But one and the same Spirit works all these things, distributing to each one individually as He wills." (Verses 10 and 11)

It clearly says, "to another prophecy", while Chapter 14 says, "you can all prophesy". They seem to contradict each other.

Does the Bible contradict itself? No, it does not. The Bible always tells the truth. Read both chapters carefully. Chapter 12 says, "distributing to each one individually as He wills", which means distributing a spiritual gift to each of us. On the other hand, Chapter 14 says, "you can all prophesy." It is not saying, "you all have 'the spiritual gift of prophecy'."

I had an opportunity to watch the Atlanta Olympic Games. I was moved by the performance of Miss Arimori, a Japanese marathon runner; she won third place. She has a special ability in running. Think of ourselves now. We can run; with a few exceptions, we all can run. However, only some people can run fast and over a long distance like Miss Arimori can. All of us can run, but certain people are given "a gift" of special running ability. Similarly, we all can prophesy, but some people are given an excellent ability in the gift of prophecy.

Let us eagerly pursue the gift of prophecy. Even if

we are not given the gift of prophecy, we can receive great benefit from prophesying.

Prophecy will be fulfilled

When prophecies began to be spoken to us about overseas missions, establishing an overseas mission office was also prophesied. When some of the church members heard about this, they felt a real burden, and organized a prayer meeting for that. They were so eager that they got together around the four main people once a week and continued praying.

But, no matter how much they prayed, they could not see any progress at all. The members dropped out one by one, but the four main members did not give up. After praying for two or three more years with still no developments, one of them had to move to England for family reasons, and two others gave up. However, the last person did not give up; this lady kept holding on to that prophecy about the overseas mission office. Finally, the overseas mission office did open, with its room provided, when it was very late from a human viewpoint, but at the most proper time from God's viewpoint.

As of September 1996, that lady was the central figure in the overseas mission office, which was later renamed "Mission Office." That lady did see the word from God fulfilled because she had held on to it firmly.

Prophecy must be examined, but if it is truly from God, it will never fail to be fulfilled. Of course, any word from God that is given in any form, other than prophecy, will surely be fulfilled if it is genuinely from Him. However, we have to continue believing it. There are many people who do not see it fulfilled because they do not believe it. We should never let go of any word coming from God if it is truly from Him, no matter how long we may have to wait or how impossible it may seem. We will see God's victory after many trials. The Lord never lies.

CHAPTER 5

Prophecy is a spiritual gift given to the church

Prophecy should be used carefully

God's work through prophecy is wonderful. Through prophecy, we are comforted, encouraged, edified, shown God's plan and given direction. The work of prophecy is very powerful.

If we were given a handgun, we would handle it carefully. Misuse of it would cause serious trouble because it is a powerful weapon. It is just same with prophecy. We have to handle prophecy with care according to the guidelines in the Bible.

We often hear of failures and problems related with prophecy. Because of this, people tend to judge that prophecy is dangerous. However, prophecy-related problems are caused by the wrong use of prophecy. When we use it properly, according to the Bible, such problems do not occur.

When I was a first-year student in seminary, I

started bleeding in the stomach and was admitted to hospital. My massive blood loss at that time required repeated blood transfusions and iron injections. The injection was to put an iron medication directly into the blood stream. It was terribly painful. The pain spread through all the blood vessels in my arm and made me feel as if my whole arm had fallen off. I have never experienced such painful injections since then. On top of that, this injection took time. The nurse injected the medication little by little, taking about twenty minutes. It was like a time of torture.

The nurse explained to me that iron medications were poisonous and that they would be dangerous if they were not injected in that way. The medication used then was very powerful; if it was injected without following set procedures it would be very dangerous.

Prophecy is a powerful weapon that God has given us. However, its misuse can cause some big problems. The important points which we should bear in mind in using prophecy are to know that the gift of prophecy belongs to the Church, and to test each prophecy to see if it is from God even when it was spoken by an excellent prophet.

Prophecy is a gift for the church

Soon after I had experienced God's work through prophecy, a friend of mine in our church told me about his interesting experience. He told me that he had been given the gift of prophecy when he was a member of another church. However, he had become proud as he used this gift. He had started to judge the pastor and the church, and had finally left the church. After that, he was badly possessed by an evil spirit. He had a missionary bound to a post to cast out the evil spirit from him, and finally, he was released.

Certainly the problem occurred, using prophecy. However, it seems that this problem was caused by two reasons: firstly, he became so proud; secondly, he left the church. We must be aware that spiritual gifts belong to the church, and that we are part of the church.

"But one and the same Spirit works all these things, distributing to each one individually as He wills. For as the body is one and has many members, but all the members of that one body, being many, are one body, so also is Christ." (1 Corinthians 12:11-12)

Verse 27 says, "Now you are the body of Christ, and members individually." Each of us is a part of Christ's body, the universal church. At the same time we are a part of a local church, a member of such and such a church. For example, I belong to and am a part of the Lord's Cross Christian Center, City of Christ Church. Each of us is a part or organ (the eye, mouth, ear, hand or whatever it may be) of Christ's body, which is each of the local churches. A spiritual gift represents the function of an organ.

If I am an eye, I am gifted with the ability of seeing. However, I myself and my gift are not something that I posses for my own benefit. Both belong to the Holy Spirit, and to Christ's body, the church. The eye may realize that it can see better than anyone else in the church, but it is nothing to boast of, because it has the function and responsibility of seeing in the body. But the eye cannot hear, because the function of hearing is given to the ear. The eye depends on the ear for hearing, and the ear on the eye for seeing, each displaying their own gifts for the other. Likewise, all of us who are parts of Christ's body depend on one another; the body works well when we contribute according to our own abilities.

What if the eye thought that it did not like the body and left it? It can neither hear nor walk. It has no eye lid to protect it, no mouth to eat with, and no stomach to digest food. Therefore, it would be suicidal for the eye to leave the body.

The function of the spiritual gifts belongs to the church. It is each of us who uses them, but they belong to the Holy Spirit, to Christ, to God and to the church. Therefore, using them independently of the church causes many problems. As 1 Corinthians 12:7 says, "But the manifestation of the Spirit is given to each one for the profit of all," so we have to be conscious that we, as parts of Christ's body, should use them for the profit of all. Using them in this way will bring wholesome, wonderful results; we will frequently see God's glory in such work.

Spiritual gifts must be used within the order of the church

In addition, we should not ignore order in the church when using spiritual gifts. In 1 Corinthians 14:39-40 it says, "Therefore, brethren, desire earnestly to prophesy, and do not forbid to speak with tongues. Let all things be done decently and in order." They say that all things are to be done in an orderly manner.

We can see that this refers particularly to tongues and prophecy as Verse 39 mentions them. Order is required for all things, particularly for work in the church through tongues and prophecy.

As a man has the head which gives commands to the rest of his body, a church also has its head. The head is, of course, Jesus Christ; we, as parts of His body, the church, obey His directions. There is order within the church, with Jesus Christ as the head.

There are some types of church government: the congregational, the Presbyterian, the Episcopal, etc.; the authority structure differs from system to system. However, in spiritual matters the authority certainly resides in the appointed pastor. The authority structure is important to maintain order in the church. Without a clear authority structure the church will become disordered.

In other words, we should follow the instructions of the pastor and obey his authority in spiritual matters, such as spiritual gifts. Most of the problems with prophecy stem from the fact that people who prophesy left the church or disobeyed its authority. Not confined to the area of spiritual gifts, it is important that we stay under the authority of the church and obey that authority.

When I say so, some of you may say, "But the pastor of my church does not allow prophecy. What should I do?" The answer is simple and clear. You should not prophesy in the church because all things should be done properly and in an orderly manner. However, pray for your pastor. Also, tell him about prophecy if you feel guided to do so. But, be careful about this; some people have put themselves in a difficult situation because they did so. However, if God leads you in that way, take up the burden of the cross and obey Him.

I have met several people who began to experience the gift of prophecy although they attended the churches which did not admit prophecy. If you find yourself in such a situation, you will sometimes have an extremely difficult time. Nevertheless, be thankful in that situation, for the Lord, knowing everything, is leading you, and obey what He says, carefully examining whether it is really from Him. However, as far as the work within your own church is concerned, you must obey the pastor.

The danger of being separated from the church

One day, a woman came to our church. She seemed to have been moving around from church to church. If you are doing the same, I would recommend that you stay at one church, which is of great importance spiritually.

This woman gave a prophecy in our church meeting. In our church, only a limited number of members are allowed to prophesy in a public service. I felt that she had a problem with submitting to church order and that what she had prophesied was not from the Lord. Of course, I could not allow her to prophesy, and stopped her from doing so in our church. I told her that if she received a prophecy she should write it on a piece of paper and give it to me, and not to speak it out.

She did that for a while but her prophecies were

still not right. Soon, she stopped coming to our church. Later, I heard that she attended another church, where an embarrassing thing happened. She started prophesying there, claiming that she had been trained in prophecy at the Lord's Cross Christian Center. The pastor of that church was troubled by her.

Through a third person I communicated to that pastor what she had been doing at our church. She may have heard about that, and got angry at me. She telephoned me and prophesied about me, saying, "You will have a big problem. You'll feel really ashamed." I knew that it was not from the Lord and, of course, did not accept it. Rather, I sensed a strong satanic power behind it.

If you come across such a situation, you should carefully examine the prophecy. If you can deal with it, that's good. Otherwise, ask your pastor for advice as he is the spiritual authority in your church. The woman eventually left that church as well, but apparently continued prophesying. A long time afterwards, I heard that she had been found dead in her apartment, one week after her death.

It is dangerous if we leave our church and prophesy outside its spiritual authority. We have to use this spiritual gift and grow in it while belonging to a church, serving the church faithfully, and submitting to the spiritual authority of the pastor. In this framework, we will be protected and prophecy will be effectively used.

If you are prophesying outside church authority, I strongly recommend that you come under the covering of a church, in whatever form that may be, as soon as possible. I have seen many people blessed, and their prophecies effectively used, when they used prophecy as a spiritual gift to the church and under the authority of the church. We have to understand that prophecy is a spiritual gift for the church. Prophecy works most effectively when it is used in a church as a gift for the church.

The blessings given when obeying God

Several years after starting our church, a prophecy was given to us that said, "A person called Che will come to your church." The prophecy went on to say, "the person will come over often." I was not familiar with the name "Che," but somebody told me that it was a Korean name, pronounced Sai in Japanese. I knew the world famous Pastor Sai, the mother of Pastor Cho Yonggi. However, it was inconceivable to me that such a famous person would come to our church. We were talking and wondering who this Sai was.

Meanwhile, the way was suddenly opened to bring Pastor Sai, the mother of Pastor Cho Yonggi, to our church. The gathering with Pastor Sai was wonderfully blessed. Our church has changed since then; what Pastor Sai said at that gathering triggered off our all-night prayer meetings every Friday night. We received wonderful blessings including advice about pastoral ministry.

After Pastor Sai had visited our church several times, I heard that she collapsed and was hospitalized. At that time, the Lord said to me through prophecy, "Pastor Sai will go to heaven. Since I have something to tell you through her, go and see her in Korea right away."

While I was wondering what to do, considering travel expenses and my busy schedule, I heard that she had left hospital and gone on a mission trip to the U.S. I thought, "What a relief! That prophecy was wrong." But, immediately after that I heard that she had gone to heaven during the U.S. trip. I missed hearing what I was supposed to hear because I did not obey.

A short while later a prophecy said, "Go and see Pastor Tetsuo Inoue(former Pastor of Akasaka Church, the United Church of Christ in Japan) immediately as he will soon pass away. I have something to tell you through him." Pastor Inoue was then in hospital, but he sometimes taught at our seminary as a lecturer. His lectures were given at his Akasaka Church so I had not met him personally. However, I did not think he would die so soon, because I had heard that he had left hospital a short while before and that he was giving lectures in good condition. So, on the day I should have been visiting him if I had obeyed the Lord, I went to a zoo with my children. I thought that I could visit him in a couple of weeks' time. Immediately after that, he went to heaven. I again failed to hear what I was supposed to hear.

We can miss some things because of our disobedience. Later, the Lord said to me through a prophecy, "Through Brother Ilie Coroama I will tell you what Pastor Sai and Pastor Inoue were going to tell you." The Lord covered up my failures. There are things the Lord is going to do through prophecy. We should experience more of His blessings through prophecy.

CHAPTER 6

Prophecy must be tested before accepting it

Testing individual prophecies

One day, I took my children to a department store. I let them enjoy themselves looking at toys in a toyshop, while I sat down on a bench in a rest area on the same floor. In that area there was a booth specially set up for drawing fortune telling lots; three monkey figurines were placed like idols, and in front of them there was a lottery machine to turn to draw the fortune telling lots.

Interestingly, all of the people waiting in the line were women; most of them were junior and senior high school students. After drawing, some of them were happy but others were unhappy with what their fortunes foretold. Then they said, "Is this really true?"; they were judging their fortunes in their own way.

Prophecy is a wonderful gift from God; we can receive His words through it. However, we should not just accept all of the words of prophecy, because 1 Corinthians 14:29 says, "Let two or three prophets speak, and let the others judge." This verse does not tell us to discern true prophets from false ones. Of course, we need to make such a distinction; however, here it is assumed that prophecy is spoken by servants of God, and then it tells us to discern whether each of their words are truly from God or not. We therefore must distinguish, judge and discern prophecies. We must test prophecies spoken even by respected prophets, by prophets who have never made a mistake, even by Billy Graham, by Yonggi Cho, or by whomever else except Jesus Christ.

In all spiritual matters, not limited to prophecy, failure to discern causes big problems. The Bible tells us to test all things, as well as saying, "Do not despise prophecies." (1 Thessalonians 5: 20)

Accepting prophecy after testing

When I visited China, a member of an underground church told me the following story: In a certain church, a prophecy was spoken, saying that Christ would come again on a particular day of a certain month and that everybody should go up to the mountain top. The prophecy went on to say, "If you take off your clothes and jump off the mountain, you will be raptured." If Christians who did not know about testing heard this prophecy, they could have come to a disastrous end.

A problem occurred in a certain church. A prophecy said, "God is leading brother A and sister B into marriage." Eventually, they decided not to get married, but they were troubled, hurt and devastated in the process. Also, the church got so afraid of prophecy that God's work through prophecy stopped. I wish they had known about testing prophecy.

There are three kinds of prophecy: one from th Holy Spirit, one from the person's mind, and one from Satan. We need to carefully discern prophecy to see if it is from God.

Chapter 22 of 1 Kings tells the story of Ahab the king of Israel and Jehoshaphat the king of Judah. Ahab asked Jehoshaphat for help and suggested to him that they fight Aram together. Jehoshaphat replied, "Please inquire for the word of the Lord today." (Verse 5) The chapter goes on to say:

"Then the king of Israel gathered the prophets together, about four hundred men, and said to them, 'Shall I go against Ramoth Gilead to fight, or shall I refrain?' So they said, 'Go up, for the Lord will deliver it into the hand of the king.' And Jehoshaphat said, 'Is there not still a prophet of the Lord here, that we may inquire of Him?'"(1Kings 22:6-7)

Ultimately, King Jehoshaphat was going to fight, but he was testing the prophecy to see if it was really from God. He later heard the correct prophecy from Micaiah, "I saw all Israel scattered on the mountains, as sheep that have no shepherd. And the Lord said, 'These have no master. Let each return to his house in peace.'" (1 Kings 22:17)

In spite of the prophecy, Jehoshaphat went to war. He probably decided to do so to fulfill his obligation to Ahab. Be that as it may, please remember that prophecies were tested also in the time of the Old Testament.

Listen to prophecy calmly

Seven or eight years ago, our first outreach team to Europe left Japan. The team was scheduled to attend a conference in Switzerland, and then go on to the communist nations of East Europe.

Many people who were attending the conference prophesied; participants of various countries were called up in turn to the platform to receive prophecy. Some cried and some others tearfully praised the Lord when they were given prophecies. Their attitude towards prophecy was extremely emotional.

We, the Japanese team, were also called upon. We were the only participants from Asia, so we stood out quite a bit. On the platform, many workers of God stood around us to pray over us, and some prophecies were spoken out. We had heard many prophecies in Japan and were getting used to them. Also, we were aware that prophecy had to be tested. On the platform we were carefully testing the prophecies that were being spoken. The people who were prophesying over us seemed to be wondering why we remained so calm. We cannot be too calm about prophecy; we should not be emotional about it. We should calmly listen to it and test it. Then, only when we are sure it was right, we should accept it.

An American friend of mine, who is a prominent prophet, once told me that he often makes mistakes in prophesying when he prays upon request. He is right.

Even though a prophet gives a wonderful prophecy, like a home run hitter, which will have come true later, he may be struck out in the next batter's box. We should carefully test each and every prophecy.

Testing directive prophecy

Testing is particularly important for directive and foretelling prophecies. Teaching prophecies also need to be tested. But from my experience, the person who speaks that kind of prophecy seldom says anything odd because he knows the Bible. Of course, if a prophecy says something unbiblical, like hating others, it should be discarded. Strictly speaking, a prophecy telling people to love others also needs to be tested, for it can be either from God or from the prophet who is speaking. However, it would not do you much harm in that case even if you couldn't test that prophecy.

On the other hand, directive and foretelling prophecies, particularly directive ones, will cause big problems if a person follows directions that are wrong. Therefore, we should be extra careful when direction and foretelling come into prophecy. We need to test such prophecy thoroughly.

About two years after the church had started, a prophecy was given. At that time, we had two worship services on Sundays, and one on Mondays. My co-worker and I were pastoring the church together under God, but I preached all the messages myself. The prophecy said, "Pastor Akimoto is to give messages in the second worship service and in the Monday service, and his co-worker in the first service." Several other prophets followed suit with similar prophecies. However, I felt very uneasy while I was listening to the prophecy. Also, I was concerned that the difference in preaching between the first and second worship services would create different, pastoral, ministry directions. I sought God's will and He stopped me from following that directive prophecy.

Several years later, I realized that my co-worker and I differed greatly in our understanding of spiritual matters, and we were separated temporarily. The church would have been greatly confused if we had followed the prophecy without testing it first. Prophecy must be tested.

Some people insist that nobody can test what "God says". However, God tells us in the Bible to test prophecy. We must do so even when prophecy is spoken in such a way that "God says," "Jesus Christ says,"or "the Holy Spirit says." Testing prophecy is the will of God.

We should test prophecies, thoroughly discern them, confirm them as being from God, and then accept and follow them. It is God who decided that prophecies should be tested.

Accepting correct prophecies only

When we went on our first mission trip to the Philippines, we were scheduled to return to Japan on Monday after three weeks of ministry. On Saturday of the previous week, a pig was brought to the church where we were staying. We had fun playing with the pig and teasing it, but the pig looked very uneasy.

Early next morning before our dawn prayer meeting, we heard a sudden, sharp squeal just outside our room. According to the person who went to scout out, the big was being strangled by a man. We then knew that the pig had been brought to be part of the feast for our farewell party after the service. The butcher had just come to slaughter it; he was so poor at his job that the pig squealed for about twenty minutes before it finally became quiet.

The whole roasted pig was served at lunch time. We were told that roast pork was considered the choicest food in that area. However, we felt a little sick and could not look at the pig; for we had played with it the previous day. Filipino brothers and sisters kindly served a variety of nice food onto our plates. Of course, "the pig" was amongst it. I felt sorry for the Filipino people, but I was careful to separate "the pig" from the other food and I enjoyed the rest of the lunch.

We must carefully distinguish prophecies between the ones that are from God and the ones that are not. Of course pork is not poisonous, but wrong prophecy is, more or less, poisonous to us. We should sort out and choose good things only. Prophecy needs testing. We should accept it only when we can be sure that it is from God after careful examination. Wrong prophecies must be discarded. If you are not sure whether a prophecy is right or wrong, keep it in the corner of your mind; don't let it influence your life. When you are sure that it is from God, then follow it.

Prophecy is a spiritual gift for the church, to be used under the authority of the church, and at the same time it always requires testing. If you work consistently within this framework, prophecy will be effectively used.

The truthfulness of the prophecy that God has given us

In June 1993 we sent a mission team to the U.S. The team was going to minister at churches in Los Angeles and Denver, and to the congregation of Elim Fellowship in the State of New York. In addition, we were expecting the new way for the overseas missions to be opened during this trip. For we had been told through prophecy, "At Rochester I am going to open the way for the overseas missions to Poland. Watch and see how it will be opened."

Long before our overseas mission activities had started, we had been given a prophecy about the mission work to Poland and had been praying for it. However, the way had been opened to countries in Asia, Europe and the U.S., but not to Poland. We had been to Poland before to pray and to wage spiritual warfare, but the door remained closed for specific activities such as contacts with Polish Christians and ministry opportunities in churches in that country.

We were scheduled to go to Elim Fellowship, about thirty minutes drive from Rochester Airport, so I expected that the way to the mission in Poland would be opened at Elim. We stayed at Elim for several days, ministering at the meetings and talking with the church leaders, but we did not see the way to the mission to Poland opened up there. We arrived at Rochester Airport, somewhat disappointed.

About fifteen minutes before our departure, when we thought we should be getting ready to board the plane, several people from Elim rushed in to see us off. They were glad to have made it in time. Among those people was a person who was once the principal of a seminary in Poland. During those few minutes of exchanging goodbyes, the way to missions in Poland was opened. It was right before we boarded the plane. Just as the Lord had said to us, "Watch and see how it will be opened," He opened it at the very last minute.

Also, the Lord had said to us, "I will open the way in Rochester." We had thought Elim was in Rochester, but it was actually in Lima, an adjacent town. Do you know where Rochester was? The airport itself was in Rochester city. What the Lord does is so wonderful. The way to the missions in Poland was really opened in Rochester just as He had told us.

At the end of November 1993 we went to Poland. We ministered at several churches and enjoyed fellowship with each other in that country, which brought us a great joy.

When there seemed to be no possibility of overseas missions, several people gathered together in a six tatami-mat room in my house and prayed earnestly for the mission to Poland. At that time it had seemed to be an impossible goal. However, the Lord kept telling us about it. Finally, in the eighth year of praying for the mission to Poland, we stood on Polish soil.

The Lord is faithful. He has fulfilled what He has said He would do. We should never make light of prophecy.

CHAPTER 7

Prophecy in
New Testament times

~~~

Prophecy is a blessing from God

Prophecy is a wonderful gift from God because He will do many wonderful things for us through it. Why not use this wonderful means of grace as Christians?

Because of my work I visit various places throughout Japan and the world. After many trips I have found an economical way to travel, at about half the usual cost (of course by lawful means). Before, I did not know about such ways and paid high costs, but not anymore. Now I use that cheaper way to travel.

The Lord has greatly blessed us through prophecy. Without using prophecy, we would have missed out on some blessings from God.

Prophecy is a wonderful gift. We should fully use this gift. However, among Christian, nothing is more misunderstood and confused in understanding than this spiritual gift. We hear so many wrong concepts: prophets must die or must be called false prophets when a prophecy they speak out does not come true, even once; prophecy has died down in this generation; prophecy is a product of occult, etc. Hearing these reports, many people may be misled and naturally come to believe that they had better not to be concerned in prophecy. However, we have to be extremely careful not to be misled because it is God and His words that we should follow. What God says is true.

The First Corinthians 14:1 says, "Pursue love, and desire spiritual gifts, but especially that you may prophesy." The Lord is surely telling us to pursue love and spiritual gifts, particularly prophecy.

Understanding the difference between the Old and New Testaments

Confusion about prophecy seems to stem from the misunderstanding of the relationship between the Old Testament and the New Testament. Both the Old and New Testaments are based on the revelations of God; we accept them both as the infallible Word of God. But sometimes we find that contents of the Old Testament on certain matters differ from those of the New Testament. In this case, we should accept the matters in the New Testament, because the Old Testament plays the role of directing us to the New Testament.

For example, during Old Testament times, people offered sacrifices of cows and sheep for the forgiveness of their sins. However, in New Testament times, people receive forgiveness by believing in the Cross of Jesus Christ. Therefore, if modern-day Christians offer sacrifices of cows and sheep in order to observe what the Old Testament says, they are making a terrible mistake. Redemption has been realized through the Cross of Jesus Christ in New Testament times.

Both the Old and New Testaments are the infallible Word of God, but when they give different revelations regarding the same matters, the New Testament takes precedence over the Old Testament.

In the seminary I graduated from, I heard there was once a student who studied the Old Testament so deeply that he was converted to Judaism. This is because, for one thing, he was not saved, but also he apparently did not know the relationship between the Old and New Testaments. We need to be aware of this relationship.

The Old and New Testaments also tell us different things about prophecy. We should accept what the New Testament says when the Old and New Testaments describe the same subject differently.

God's people in the Old and New Testaments

Before discussing prophecy as described in the Old and New Testaments, we need to understand the basic differences between God's people in the Old Testament times and those in the New Testament times.

First, in Old Testament times, the Holy Spirit did not abide in each of the people of God but only in a limited number of people like prophets or kings. However, after Pentecost, the Holy Spirit abides in all people who believe in Jesus Christ. Second, in Old Testament times, the Bible was unavailable to the people. For most of that time, even the Old Testament had not been completed, not to mention the New Testament. We can now study God's teachings and works, and discern through the Old and New Testaments. However, in Old Testament times, because of the incompleteness of the Bible, people were in a very poor situation concerning the knowledge of God and discernment.

Also, we learn and discern by the Holy Spirit (1 John 2:27, and 1 Corinthians 12:10), but in Old Testament times the Holy Spirit did not abide in the people of God. Therefore, in those times, when a prophet prophesied, the people's ability to discern prophecy was very poor because they did not have the Holy Spirit abiding in them, and the Bible as a basis of testing was not completed. Because of this, if a prophet made an error, there was a strong possibility that all the people would stumble over what he prophesied.

However, in New Testament times, the discerning ability of each one of us is sufficiently strong and in no way can it be compared to that of the Old Testament people. For we have the Old and New Testaments, which are the completed revelation of God, and also, the Holy Spirit abides in each one of us.

The responsibility of prophets in
Old Testament times

You may notice when you read the Old and New Testaments that the Old Testament stresses the responsibility of the prophet, while the New Testament stresses the responsibility on the part of the listeners to discern the prophecy.

Deuteronomy 18:20 says, "But the prophet who presumes to speak a word in My name, which I have not commanded him to speak, or who speaks in the name of other gods, that prophet shall die."

A prophet speaking in the name of other gods is obviously a false prophet. The verse also mentions a prophet speaking out something in God's name that God did not tell him to say. The Holy Spirit is not in such a prophet. That prophet is just speaking out his own dreams, visions and thoughts as he wishes.

Verses 21 and 22 describe the key to testing: "And if you say in your heart, 'How shall we know the word which the Lord has not spoken?'—when a prophet speaks in the name of the Lord, if the thing does not happen or come to pass, that is the thing which the Lord has not spoken; the prophet has spoken it presumptuously; you shall not be afraid of him." If what the prophet said was not fulfilled, he was a false prophet and had to be put to death.

In Old Testament times, true prophets did not make mistakes in their prophecy; they clearly stood out from prophets who made mistakes in prophecy. The Holy Spirit was only in true prophets, and not in "prophets" who had ever made a mistake in prophecy. This is very different from the situation in New Testament times.

Responsibility of testing in New Testament times

In New Testament times the Holy Spirit abides in each one of us. The Bible advises that every one of us should prophesy, and at the same time, it tells us to judge prophecy.

It is just as 1 Corinthians 14:29 says, "Let two or three prophets speak, and let the others judge." This verse is not telling us to examine prophets; it is telling us to examine prophecies. Here, it is assumed that that some prophecies in New Testament times may contain errors. We, of course, have to distinguish true prophets from false ones in New Testament times, too. But we have to examine each prophecy because some prophecies spoken out, even by true prophets, can be wrong. We Christians can test prophecies because the Holy Spirit abides in each one of us, and the Old and New Testaments, which are the basis of our testing, have been completed.

When I was a seminary student, I usually had breakfast with fellow students; a bowl of soup was often served. One day, just as I was about to eat my soup, I found unusual things in the soup. There were a lot of tiny insects floating together with the vegetables. When I tried to remove the insects, a girl student said to me in a low voice, "Eat it as it is, otherwise you'll upset the lady who cooked the meal." I quickly ate up the soup, but I felt like I was drinking poison.

In the case of prophecy, this sort of attitude is not right. We have to distinguish right from wrong, no matter what others may think, because God is telling us to do so. Of course, it does not mean that prophets can say anything. They have to try their best not to make mistakes when they are prophesying. On the other hand, we, the listeners, have to test prophecies without fail.

Mistakes are allowed

Many people have a misunderstanding about prophets. They think true prophets never make a mistake in prophesying, not even one mistake.

One day, I had an opportunity to talk with a Korean woman who prophesied. She gave a word of foretelling prophecy to my wife when she was single. The prophecy said, "You will get married to a pastor." That prophecy certainly came true.

While talking to her, I explained briefly that any prophet could make a mistake in New Testament times. The moment I said this, her face lit up, and she said, "I can't tell you how much I have been worried about that, but I understand now."

Prophecies in Old Testament and New Testament times have some things in common, but differ greatly in other respects.

Accurate prophecies

In 1988, we were given a directive prophecy telling us to go to the U.S. We prayed and tested it in many respects, and the prophecy was eventually confirmed when we received an invitation to the U.S. from a chaplain of the U.S. Air Force, and when we received some money for travel. So, we went to the U.S. in July.

Before leaving Japan, we were given some more prophecies about this trip. One of the prophecies foretold that we would meet two important people, and that one of them already knew about us and was praying for us. We met one of them, Brother R., without any

73

problems, but the other person, Brother I., was on a trip abroad and it seemed it would be impossible to meet him. However, no sooner had he returned from abroad than he came to meet us.

Brother R. said to us, "I haven't told Brother I. anything about you, but he has heard from God and knows a lot about you. Why don't you ask him?" When we asked him when we met him, he told us several things about us, starting with the comment: "You are people of prayer, aren't you?" We were surprised to find that he had known about us and that he had been praying for us. Later on, we learned many things through Brother R. and Brother I.

Another prophecy given to us before this trip said, "The Lord will give you a sudden, unexpected guidance on this trip. Pray so that you can obey Him." One more prophecy was given, saying, "This U.S. team will go to Mexico. You'll be preaching there." I could not believe that one because we didn't have any tickets to Mexico and we had never been there, and even more, we didn't know anybody there and we didn't have any contacts with any churches in that country.

Brother R. lived in Waco, near Dallas. He kindly put us up there, and taught us the Bible from early in the morning (However, we were so tired that most of us dozed off). At the lunch time, he talked about churches in Mexico. Then he suddenly proposed that we go to Mexico together. When we asked if it was really possible, he said that it was worth a try. We began to wonder if we should really go, but we finally decided to give it a go in spite of opposition from some members, because it might be the "sudden guidance by the Spirit." That evening, we were all aboard a plane bound for Mexico.

Brother R. was well known in Mexico. When we arrived in Mexico that night, the pastor of the church was very pleased to meet us. From the next day on, meetings were held three times a day. Brother R, after he delivered his message at the first meeting, came up to me and said, "The Holy Spirit is telling me to ask you to preach." Incredibly, God suddenly led us to Mexico and I was preaching in Mexico as He had said. The Lord is alive; he did what he told us He would do.

Prophecy against danger

Also, this team had been given a prophecy against danger, which foretold: " Either you or Brother T. will be involved in a traffic accident. It will definitely happen, so pray." We started praying earnestly.

One evening several days before we left for Japan, Brother T. was travelling in a car with some American evangelists. The car was speeding along the expressway when it brushed against a truck beside it and went into a spin. The moment it was heading towards a cliff, the car suddenly regained control. It was truly amazing. Nothing could account for it except the Lord's intervention. Such incidents usually develop into serious, often fatal, accidents. However, nobody was injured, not even Brother T. I heard that the American evangelists were excitedly saying, "It's a miracle! It's a miracle!"

God had forewarned us against the traffic accident. He saved us through prayer. God is alive. God's love,

His guidance and works are real. Prophecy is a great blessing God uses for our benefit. We should not be indifferent to this blessing of prophecy.

CHAPTER 8

Testing based on the Bible

🖋️

God's work through prophecy is wonderful. However, there is one absolute requirement when using prophecy: it must be used biblically.

The other day, I bought an electric appliance. Its instruction manual warned users not to handle it with wet hands, because of the danger of getting an electric shock. Prophecy is a wonderful spiritual gift, but we have to use it in the right way. In other words, we must use it biblically or we will see many people get electric shocks. We should avoid the shocks.

Testing is for both the church and individuals

The Bible says that prophecy is a spiritual gift for the church. Therefore, we have to use prophecy under the supervision of the church.

The Bible also says that we have to judge prophecy. The judges are the church and the individuals who listen to prophecy. The First Corinthians 12:10 says, "to another discerning of spirits". This spiritual gift which is given for the church discerns. This gift is very powerful for discerning whether a prophecy came from the Spirit of God, from man or from Satan. Also, the Lord has appointed pastors for the church. God has provided the church with discernment as part of her function. Therefore, the church has to judge prophecies.

In addition, individuals also have to judge prophecies as 1 Corinthians 14:29 says, "Let two or three prophets speak, and let the others judge." None of us should accept prophecies without examining them. The judges are the church and individuals.

The basis of testing is the Bible

The basis of testing prophecy is the Bible, which is the completed revelation of God. Prophecy is not and cannot be new revelation. Prophecy stays within the framework of teachings written in the Bible. Any prophecy outside this framework is not from God. We should definitely reject it.

One day, a woman gave me a copy of the Japanese translation of the prophecy spoken by a Jewish Christian, saying that a wonderful prophecy was given. However, the prophecy was wrong because it described the future of the Jews, the Palestinians and the Palestinian State differently from those written in the Bible. Prophecy must be consistent with the Biblical descriptions and teachings. It also should be used in the way that is written in the Bible.

A man once came to our church. He told us that our way of prophesying was wrong and then he left.

He had seen the style of prophecy several times, where a person stands up and prophesies. He said that our way of prophesying was different from that. In our church, several prophets prophesy in turn. This way of prophesying is based on 1 Corinthians 14:29 which says, "Let two or three prophets speak" and Verse 31 which says, "For you can all prophesy one by one". This is the way described in the Bible. We have to be careful about what the Bible says.

Bible and experience

There seem to be two types of Christians, regardless of whether or not they are involved in charismatic activities like prophesying. One type bases their actions on the Bible, and the other type on their experiences.

In my Christian life I personally have experienced many spiritual phenomena. I was able to understand most of the phenomena biblically. However, there were some that I could not; I am certain they were from God, but I could not explain them through the Bible.

If you have such experiences, I would advise you not to pursue them. I do not deny such experiences as they are real to those who have had. However, if we cannot understand them through the Bible, we must not go ahead with them. Acting out of experiences is dangerous, because it may lead us away from or against the Bible without realizing it. It is particularly dangerous for people with charismatic gifts to act out of their experiences without fully confirming them through the Bible.

When I was a little boy, my family used to go

to a public bath-house on Sunday evenings. A public bathhouse was sort of a place for social interaction where we could see our neighbors. I have many good old memories about that place. On our way to and from the bath-house, my younger brother, while looking up at the sky, often claimed that the moon was always following him. Since I already had a scientific knowledge about it, I repeatedly told him that it only appeared to be like that. However, he stubbornly refused to accept it.

The moon really appeared to be following me while I was walking and looking up at the sky. If my brother had not learned science later, he might have believed the idea that came out of his own experience all through his life. That is an illusion. We have to be careful about it. Our experiences and senses are not reliable. If we rely on them, it is not an exaggeration to say that we will, without fail, be led astray.

Danger of experientialism

There was a person in our church who was especially gifted in the discerning of spirits. He was not only able to discern them, but also to see them and feel the presence of them. However, he gradually began to avoid evil spirits. He probably was repelled or horrified by them. From previous experience it is natural for people to want to avoid a savage, wild dog in their path and to take a different route. However, we should not act like this toward Satan. I do not think that it is a good idea to dare to deal with Satan ourselves unless it is the will of the Lord. However, the Bible tells us to resist him as 1 Peter 5:9 says, "Resist him, steadfast in the faith." It does not tell us to flee from him or avoid him. Therefore, we must oppose Satan because the Bible says so. If you act out of your experiences, you will tend to handle such things in a manner contrary to the Bible.

Among evangelicals are some who claim that divine healing and tongues no longer exist based on the fact that they haven't experienced those, not putting that explicitly. When they try to interpret the Bible according to their experience, many contradictions will result. Whether we have experienced spiritual phenomena or not, we should not rely on experientialism based on instances of what we have or have not gone through. Rather, we should focus on being the Bible-based.

We are entering a time of Revival; we are going to see many spiritual manifestations, healings and miracles. However, I expect various problems will arise along the way. Please be aware that experientialism holds a danger in itself.

I believe that the Evangelical stream should be based more on the Bible, but the Charismatic and Pentecostal streams should be much more so, for they deal more frequently with a wider range of spiritual phenomena. I believe this because the Bible is the one and only infallible Word of God, the completed revelation of God, which protects us.

Biblical or not

Prophecies, first of all, must be tested on the basis

of the Bible. If they are not in line with the Bible or are against it, they must be discarded.

Let me tell you a story I once heard. I do not know if it really happened, as this kind of story is often exaggerated or totally changed from what really happened. However, what this story tells could really happen, so we will take it up to learn from it. It is about an evangelist whose wife did not obey the Lord. She was warned many times through prophecy, but did not repent and kept interfering with the Lord's work. Finally, a prophecy was given to the evangelist that said, "Divorce your wife and marry a woman who follows the Lord." He obeyed this prophecy (perhaps for the sake of the Lord's work).

This is quite an elementary case of testing of prophecy. The Bible says, "whoever divorces his wife, except for sexual immorality, and marries another, commits adultery;"(Matthew 19:9) Therefore, that prophecy is obviously contrary to the Bible. He should not have divorced his wife even though she interfered with the Lord's work or did not obey Him. This prophecy was not from God. It must have been from an evil spirit or the speaker's own mind.

We should not accept the prophecies which are unbiblical or contrary to the Bible. The first step in examining prophecies is to see whether they are biblical or not. If they are unbiblical or contrary to the Bible, we should immediately reject them.

However, it does not necessarily mean that we can accept prophecies because they are biblical. Testing by the Bible is like the starting block for testing. Just standing on the starting block is not enough. We should continue testing them until we reach the goal. We have to test them from more than one aspect. We should not accept them until we have positively confirmed that they are from God.

We should remember that prophecy cannot go beyond the Bible or add anything new to the Bible. Prophecy is not and cannot be a new revelation. Prophecy is a spiritual gift that is to be used within the scope of the Bible, the completed revelation of God.

Prophecies that cannot be judged by the Bible alone

Some time ago, we were alarmed by a prophecy that said, "A Unification Church activist will try to infiltrate your church, so pray." This type of prophecy cannot be tested through the Bible only. Of course, what this prophecy says is neither unbiblical nor contrary to the Bible. However, this does not necessarily mean that what it says is right.

I first judged that it was within the scope of the Bible, and then I examined it spiritually. I sensed that it did not come from Satan and that it wasn't the speaker's idea. Spiritually, the prophecy sounded like it was from God. Also, I felt the Holy Spirit urging me to pray. I started praying about it, but I was not 100 percent sure that the prophecy was right. However, I thought that we needed to prepare for it if there was any possibility of danger.

I recommend that you pray and be prepared if you receive a warning prophecy that is possibly from God, because praying and being prepared will not harm you in the least, even if the prophecy is not from God. Also, it will protect you from ignoring God's warning if that is what it is.

One Sunday, during the period when we had been praying about this matter, a man about 50 years old and a woman about 30 years old came to our church. When I greeted them, I felt something wrong with them. However, I was put fully at ease by their introduction that they were from a Holiness Church. They started to come to our church every week, and on their own initiative they began to attend student prayer meetings in the church, claiming that they had a burden for evangelizing students.

At that time, a woman who was a member of our church came to me. She had formerly been a member of the Unification Church. According to her, the man was in a leadership position in the Unification Church. When he was questioned closely, he told lies and tried to excuse himself, but it became evident that her information was correct. That was a close call. They came under false pretences in an attempt to lead students in our church out into their movement. The Lord had informed us in advance so we had been praying about it.

I advise you to pray when you are warned through prophecy about dangers, problems or difficulties, except when the prophecy is clearly not from God.

Protection from danger and problems

Warning from the Lord is, in most cases, His grace to prepare us for danger and problems, or to help us avoid them. When we visited Europe as a team, a fore-telling prophecy said, "You will get pick pocketed in

Rome, so pray." During that three-week trip we were scheduled to visit four countries and to stay two nights in Rome. We had earnestly prayed that we would be protected from pickpockets, but then forgot all about it when we arrived in Rome. This was because there were only two men in the team, including myself, and we, men had tough time, carrying many pieces of luggage for other team members, and had no room for thinking something else. We two men were following far behind the other members of the group.

Suddenly, a group of Italian girls, who seemed to be about senior high school age, came up to the two of us. They were holding pieces of cardboard in front of them, and surrounded us. Just then, a woman from the team ran back to us and shouted at the girls, "What are you doing?" and knocked the cardboard up into the air. At that point of time, the waist porch of the male member was opened and his purse was about to be snatched. The girls were a gang of pickpockets. We had been warned about pickpockets and were praying against them. Just as we had been warned, we got pick pocketed in Rome, but were protected. It was because we had been praying about it and the Lord protected us. When God speaks to us about something, we should not treat it lightly. What the Lord says about warnings, promises, guidance or whatever will certainly come true. He does so out of His grace. We will see the outpouring of His grace when we hold on to His word.

CHAPTER 9

Ways of testing each type of prophecy Part 1

❧

The Bible is the starting block for testing

The following incident happened when we visited the Philippines for overseas missions. We were scheduled to go to Davao City in Mindanao Island via Manila, the capital of the country. We were going to take an international flight to Manila, and a domestic flight of the same airline to Davao. Airline staff at the counter in Narita Airport told us that the baggage was booked to go directly to Davao and would not need to be checked out and in again at Manila. At first I thought that it was convenient, but later I began to feel uneasy because on previous trips I had to collect my baggage at Manila, take it through Customs and check it in again at the domestic flight counter.

I told the team members about this, but everybody said that I did not need to worry because airline counter staff is professionals on this matter. Just the same, my uneasy feeling did not go away. When we arrived at Manila, I went to the baggage claim area and found our baggage coming out, one by one, on a conveyor belt. It was a close call. If we had believed what the counter staff had said, our baggage would still have been in Manila when we arrived at Davao. We might have lost it for good.

Discernment is needed for everything. If we don't test, we may invite terrible failures. In our case, what the airline counter staff member, a professional, said was wrong. We must not neglect examinations. In the area of prophecy, discernment is needed even more. Prophecy should be accepted only after testing. The basis for testing is the Bible. It is important to check if the prophecy is according to what the Bible says or not. However, it does not mean that it is all there is in discerning a prophecy. The Bible is, in most cases, just the starting block for discernment.

Testing prophecies of instruction, comfort or exhortation

Let us divide prophecies into three categories to learn about discernment in further detail. The first category includes prophecies which instruct, comfort or exhort. Prophecies in this category are very unlikely to invite problems. They are based on the teachings of the Bible, and so they would not cause a big problem even if they did not come from God. For example, a prophecy telling us to love others will not cause any big problem even if it is from the speaker's mind and not from the Holy Spirit, because it is nevertheless a teaching of the Bible. Many among the churches which allow prophecy permit prophecies of this category as it is safe.

Strictly speaking, however, prophecies of this category can come from three different sources: the Spirit of God; the speaker's mind; and Satan or an evil spirit. Therefore, we cannot rule out the possibility of inviting some dangers if we easily accept those prophecies. We also have to test them.

The speaker's own idea spoken as a prophecy will interfere with the Spirit of God and prophecies spoken by Satan or an evil spirit will work against the Holy Spirit. For example, what if a prophecy says, "Go and preach the Gospel," which was immediately followed by another prophecy, "It's time for fellowship with the Lord now. Be quiet, and seek to love Him." They are both biblical, but they are telling us opposite things. In this case, either of them was spoken by the speaker or by Satan or an evil spirit; or it is possible that neither of them was from God. Therefore, we must thoroughly test prophecies.

Various ways of discernment

As far as prophecies about the church are concerned, the pastor of the church is responsible for discerning them; as for personal prophecies, the individual. However, every individual is in a different stage and condition of spiritual growth so it is best for an individual to test prophecies with the help of the church.

Suppose the two prophecies mentioned in the previous section are given to a church. The pastors need to check if God has spoken the same thing in some other ways. Have you received the same thing through the Word, prayers, circumstances, prophecy spoken by another person, or some other way? If you have received the same thing in other ways, the possibility that the prophecy is from the Lord increases. In addition, the pastor should prayerfully think about the steps God has led the church to take until now, the direction in which God is leading the church, and the current circumstances of the church. If these elements tie in with one of the prophecies, there is a strong possibility that the prophecy is from God.

Moreover, the pastor needs to know the spiritual condition of the persons speaking the prophecy: what kinds of theories do they have? That needs to be checked in advance, for they often speak out of their own thinking. Also, for testing, the pastor needs to know if they are obedient to or critical of the church.

It is of course necessary to discern spiritually. Also, a sense to distinguish good and evil is important as Hebrews 5:14 says, "But solid food belongs to those who are of full age, that is, those who by reason of use have their senses exercised to discern both good and evil." You should prayerfully test prophecies from those aspects and ask and listen to the Lord.

If you have clear confirmation and a strong conviction from these discerning processes, then follow what the prophecy says. But if you are not really sure that the prophecy is from God, then you shouldn't accept it.

Foretelling prophecy

The second category covers foretelling prophecy. The Lord foretells in various ways including prophecy. In Acts 11, verses 27-28 say, "And in these days prophets came from Jerusalem to Antioch. Then one of them, named Agabus, stood up and showed by the Spirit that there was going to be a great famine throughout all the world, which also happened in the days of Claudius Caesar." God is omniscient. He, in the midst of His works, tells Christians what will happen in the future.

In 1994, I was told several times that I would go to Norway. However, I hadn't been to Scandinavia and I didn't have any acquaintances in Norway although I had been to Europe several times. I didn't have any means to visit Norway for missions and I had no idea how the way would be opened.

In February 1994, I was invited to a conference in India to be one of the speakers for a seminar of two thousand pastors and for a crusade meeting of five thousand people. Among the speakers there was a preacher from Norway. I thought that he might be the contact person, but I did not make any effort to contact him. After the conference, the Norwegian preacher wanted to see me. When I went to see him with my interpreter, he told me that he wanted to invite me to his church in Norway.

In June that year, just as God had foretold, I visited Norway with a team from our church. God did what he had said He would do. I did nothing, but He arranged for me to meet a pastor from Norway, and opened the way to that country through him. The Lord is alive, and His ways are perfect.

In July 1986, we went to the U.S. as a mission team for the first time. It was an audacious trip as nobody in the team could speak English, and none of us had visited the country before. During the trip, a prophecy was given. It said that a policeman would be involved in giving us help.

One Saturday we drove to Calvary Chapel, which was about two hours from our lodgings. The car was in bad condition and had already stopped a couple of times. It finally stopped dead about ten minutes after we had started driving on our way back. We hit it and banged it but nothing helped to get it to move. We called our lodging house for help, but they said they could do nothing to help.

At midnight, we were all alone in the car on a dangerous U.S. expressway. Never before had we repented and prayed so earnestly to God for help. Around 2:00 a.m., a patrol car came along, and we explained the situation to the policeman by gestures. He seemed to understand the situation. He got into our car and turned the key. To our surprise, the engine started. Of course, we had turned the key dozens of times, but the engine had not turned over at all. It was amazing. We had been helped by a policeman as it had been foretold. We got back to our lodgings safely, and we found out the next day that it had been special help from God.

A qualified mechanic thoroughly checked our car the next day, and his conclusion was that the car should not have moved even an inch with about twenty broken parts in its engine. The mechanic said that it had really been a miracle that the car had moved. The leader of Youth With a Mission, who had provided us with accommodation, gave the testimony of this miracle to his fellow members with astonishment.

Unbiblical prophecy

God foretells; foretelling is an important function of prophecy. This type of prophecy is characteristically harder to test than teaching prophecies.

Not so long ago, a prophecy was given in Korea that the Second Coming of the Lord would take place at a specific time on a particular day in a certain month, although I have forgotten the exact time and date. People there believed it, told others about it and prepared themselves for it. Even I received one of their notices. On the day, the church was surrounded by TV cameras, and church members gathered at the church and kept praising and praying. Soon the specified time came, but nothing happened. It was a striking sight that the church members were leaving the church building in deep disappointment. They had not thoroughly examined the prophecy.

Matthew 24:36 says, "But of that day and hour no one knows, not even the angels of heaven, but My Father only." Nobody knows the day and the hour. When the prophecy specified the day and the hour, it was unbiblical, and they should have disregarded it. It was a basic mistake.

Prophecies that cannot be clearly confirmed

Even a foretelling prophecy is easily discerned when it is not biblical. However, a foretelling prophecy is hard to discern when we cannot definitely say that it is not biblical. It is important to use the sense of distinguishing good and evil as described in Hebrews 5:14 and to ask God in prayer. Also, if the same thing as what a prophecy says is shown in a different way, it will be a good help for testing. It is good if you can confirm a prophecy through these means, and be convinced of it. However, if you cannot, I suggest that you store it in the back of your mind. Just leave it in the back of your mind without being influenced by it or denying it, except when the prophecies are strongly directional, or when you need by all means to confirm them.

If the Lord really foretold it, it will be fulfilled in due time. Otherwise, it will not be fulfilled. You can judge by the consequences whether it is true or false. Blindly believing an uncertain prophecy may cause problems, but denying it without confirmation is not a very good idea, either. If the prophecy is not clearly confirmed I would suggest that you store it in the back of your mind.

Foretelling prophecy about the mission trip to Vietnam

It was before Vietnam was opened to foreign visitors that a prophecy was given to me which said, "You will go to Vietnam". I sensed it might be from the Lord, but I kept it in the back of my mind because I was not confident of it. Later, we received some other words of prophecy as well as signs other than prophecy to the same effect. Brother A., who was travelling around the world carrying a cross, came to our church after Vietnam had been opened to visitors. He shared his testimony with us about his mission to Vietnam, and recommended that we go on the mission to Vietnam. We didn't have any ways at all to go to Vietnam, but the way opened to us. The Lord is faithful, and I visited Vietnam as the prophecy had said I would. We were led to an underground church there. We smuggled in Bibles and ministered at a secret meeting place. Pastor B. of the underground church and many others had an experience of spending time in prison.

A short while after we returned, I received a letter from the pastor's wife. The letter was asking me to pray for the pastor because he was ill. We thought that he was really ill, but the real intent of the letter was to tell us that the pastor had been imprisoned again. After the pastor had been released at the end of two-year imprisonment, we visited the country again. At our reunion, Pastor B. shared with us his testimony of how he had led 60 prisoners to salvation during his imprisonment. Now he and his church members are good friends of ours, and their church and ours are in a good cooperative relationship. In the future we are going to further develop this relationship.

When I was given only the word: "You will go to Vietnam," I knew nothing about what would follow. However, God who led and guided us had had a wonderful plan for us. The Lord is sincere and faithful. We should never disregard His Word.

CHAPTER 10

Ways of testing each type of prophecy Part 2

❧

God works specifically

It was when I read the life story of George Mueller that I began to realize that God leads and guides us specifically. George Mueller was a vessel of God who achieved great work by obeying His voice, even though he was not a Christian blessed with charismatic gifts. I was surprised to find in the book how God guided him with specific instructions and how He answered his prayers. This book opened up a spiritual door before me.

Acts 16:6-10 describe how the Lord specifically guides people:

"Now when they had gone through Phrygia and the region of Galatia, they were forbidden by the Holy Spirit to preach the word in Asia. After they had come to Mysia, they tried to go into Bithynia, but the Spirit did not permit them. So passing by Mysia, they came down to Troas. And a vision appeared to Paul in the night. A man of Macedonia stood and pleaded with him, saying, 'Come over to Macedonia and help us.' Now after he had seen the vision, immediately we sought to go to Macedonia, concluding that the Lord had called us to preach the gospel to them."

We can see that God gave directions to Paul in various ways. God also speaks to us and gives us directions.

In the last chapter we learned about ways of testing different types of prophecies: firstly, prophecies of instruction, comfort and exhortation; secondly, fore-telling prophecies. Now, thirdly, let us learn about testing of directive prophecy.

God gives us directions through prophecy

Prophecy is one of the main ways God gives us directions. In Judges 4:6-7 the Scripture says:

"Then she sent and called for Barak the son of Abinoam from Kedesh in Naphtali, and said to him, "Has not the Lord God of Israel commanded, 'Go and deploy troops at Mount Tabor; take with you ten thousand men of the sons of Naphtali and of the sons of Zebulun; and against you I will deploy Sisera, the commander of Jabin's army, with his chariots and his multitude at the River Kishon; and I will deliver him into your hand'?" (Judges 4:6-7)

Through the prophet Deborah, the Lord gave directions to them to go and deploy troops at Mount Tabor.

In the New Testament, Acts 13:2 says as follows:

"As they ministered to the Lord and fasted, the

Holy Spirit said, 'Now separate to Me Barnabas and Saul for the work to which I have called them.'"

Verse 1 says, "...there were certain prophets and teachers....," indicating that there were prophets on the spot. In addition, Verse 2 says, "they," showing that the Holy Spirit spoke to several people there. Therefore, this message must have been given through prophecy. The Lord gave directions to Saul and Barnabas through prophecy, to set about the work He had called them to.

Our first directive prophecy

The first directive prophecy spoken at our church was very disconcerting. A woman, whom I was praying for, suddenly began to speak out a prophecy. She said, "Mrs. A. is going to kill her son. Go and stop her." Mrs. A. was the woman's grandmother who lived in Fukuoka with her son (the woman's uncle). When I heard the prophecy I did not know what to do. If Mrs. A. was living in Tokyo where I was, it would have been easy to visit her. However, as she was in Fukuoka, it would be a big waste of time and money to visit her if the prophecy was wrong. However, I could not let the matter slide because it was a matter of life or death. I prayed to God for confirmation, but did not receive any clear answer. However, as I could not rule out the possibility that the prophecy was from the Lord, I decided that the woman should visit Mrs. A. in Fukuoka for a talk.

When the woman spoke to her grandmother about it, her grandmother was surprised and said, "How did you know that?" The woman answered, "God told me about it." The grandmother said, "That's the real God," and she believed in Jesus Christ there and then.

The grandmother had been on the point of killing her alcoholic son, and then committing suicide. Later, I baptized the grandmother, who is now in heaven. God gives directions; we will see His glory when we walk according to His directions.

Prophecy directing changes in pastoral ministry

However, nothing involves more risks than (What people think is) "directions of God" when we obey them without examining them.

A missionary, who had just arrived in Japan, went to a restaurant. He found on the table a small bottle of "coffee." He opened the bottle and emptied it in a single gulp, but immediately spat it out because it tasted terrible. Later, he learned that it was soy sauce. We often make mistakes because we do not discern. However, we should not do so regarding prophecy. The Bible tells us to "judge" (1 Corinthians 14:29).

Once I had an opportunity to give a message in Mexico. After the message, several people prayed for me. During the prayer time a very upsetting prophecy was spoken out. It said that our church was going to split and the church members were going to die spiritually. It was implicitly suggesting that we change our methods of pastoral ministry, although it did not directly say so. They prayed that our church would not fall into such a situation, but I was in a panic.

In prayer I earnestly asked the Lord what the prophecy was all about. The Lord reminded me of a couple of things about it. Firstly, the prophecy was not in line with what the Lord had told me up until then. Secondly, I did not feel spiritually that it had come from the Lord; rather I felt it was from the spirit of man. Eventually, I did not accept the prophecy.

Later, the work of our church expanded considerably, which was opposite to what that prophecy had said. Now, my conclusion is that the prophecy at that time was spoken out of the ill feeling that the speaker (he was not a Mexican, by the way) had towards us and the Japanese in general or that it was a word caused by an evil spirit which used his ill feeling. We have to examine prophecy carefully.

The Bible is the first step in examining directive prophecy

Examining directive prophecy is basically the same as examining other types of prophecy and other forms of directions from God. However, we need to be more careful with it.

The first step in examining a directive prophecy is to see whether it is contrary to the Bible or not, and to see if the prophecy is within the framework of biblical teaching. However, we often cannot tell if it is biblical because directive prophecy is more concrete and specific. For example, if it says, "Go to the United States," it is difficult to judge whether it is biblical or not because the Bible does not mention that country. To judge whether a directive prophecy is biblical or not, we need to check that the use of the prophecy is biblical and that what the prophecy says is within the framework of the Biblical teachings. (Note, however, that biblical examination is just the first step.)

One day, a pastor shared with me one of his experiences. He had been prophesying, and then one day unusual instructions started to come. For example, a prophecy said, "Go out now. Sister A. is coming." When he went out he saw Sister A. coming. Another prophecy said, "Go to the prayer room of the church. Brother B. is praying there." When he went there, he found Brother B. praying. At first he thought it was wonderful. However, a question soon came into his mind, "Does God say such things?" The Bible certainly tells us that when God speaks, He does so with a definite purpose. God never uses prophecy just to help someone guess correctly.

Later the pastor stopped prophesying. I do not think he should have stopped. I think, however, that after examining prophecy, he needed to reject bad ones. Prophecy is either from the Spirit of God, from the spirit or the mind of man, or from the evil spirit, Satan. This prophecy was from another spirit, an evil spirit.

Before eating, first remove the poison

When I was a small boy, my father took me to a Japanese restaurant to enjoy blowfish dish. At that time, I was too little to appreciate its value. I just remember that I had thinly-sliced raw fish arranged on a plate. I would be much more impressed if I had it now. Some people think that we should not eat blowfish because of its poison. However, we can eat it safely by completely removing its poison. I'll rather eat it with its poison removed, for it is delicious and highly nutritious.

I think this also holds true for prophecy. Even if there are some problems, we should experience how amazing prophecy is by removing them. We should fully examine directive prophecy and accept only that which is from God.

Other forms of signs, especially material confirmation

A key in testing a directive prophecy is found in other forms of signs by God. In other words we should see whether God has revealed the same thing through His Word, circumstances or other prophecies. Other forms of signs for the same thing will increase the possibility that the prophecy is from God. It is also important to discern it by asking God for confirmation in prayer along with the spiritual gift and the senses trained by practice to discern good and evil.

In the case of directive prophecy, material confirmation is also an important point in testing. For example, if I was given a prophecy which said, "Go to Argentina," I could not visit that country without an invitation from an Argentine church; I would also need air-travel and accommodation expenses. If these material requirements are met, then that is a good confirmation that the prophecy telling me to go to Argentina is right. Evidence like this is an important element in testing prophecy. When God directs us, He gives us everything we need and shows us everything we need to know, just as when we send our children to buy something we give our children the money for it and show them as to where the shop is located.

However, some people make light of material evidence. They say, "Because I have been told to go to Argentina, I will go by faith even though nothing has been provided." We should be very careful in a case like this because it often results in failure. The Lord sometimes directs us to go out even when there is no material confirmation. However, we should have strong confidence in such a case; besides, such a case is very rare. From personal experience, my examination of prophecy has improved greatly in accuracy since I began confirming through material evidence.

Another important element is whether or not the Holy Spirit gives us peace. Uneasiness can sometimes be a caution from the Holy Spirit. It is important to check these elements in prayer, and to test prophecy with the assistance of the church.

You need to take extra care with directive prophecy. If you are not completely sure in your own mind, never follow a directive prophecy until it has been confirmed to be right. Concentrate on your daily work and do not let the prophecy influence you. Keep it in the back of your mind, even though it may not be confirmed to be right for a long time. Don't let it overwhelm you by thinking that you are not following what the Lord has said. God is not a problem setter from a quiz show. He will never say, "Guess if this is my will or not." When God gives directions, He will clearly tell us what we are to do, because He is the one who has initiated the whole thing.

When we follow His directions

In 1985, a directive prophecy was given to me, saying, "Go to Korea and fast and pray for seven days in Pastor Yong-gi Cho's prayer cave." The Lord said to me, "Your body won't be able to stand the future work, so I am going to strengthen it through prayer and fasting."

It was true that I had been hospitalized six times, operated on three times and on the verge of death twice. I thought that the prophecy was appropriate spiritually, and I had both time and money available to travel to Korea. I thought that the fasting and praying was His will, but praying in Pastor Cho's prayer cave seemed impossible. I knew Pastor Cho, but he did not know me. Besides, he was a pastor of a church with some tens of thousands of people. Honestly, I couldn't see how it would be possible for me to use Pastor Cho's personal prayer cave. However, the Lord told me through prophecy: "Pastor Cho's prayer cave is mine. I'm going to let you use it."

Visiting Pastor Cho's church in Korea, I asked a church staff member about using the prayer cave, but he changed the subject. I thought then that I would be refused and was about to give it up. However, I dared to repeat my request to him several times because it was the Lord who had told me. Finally, he said to me with a puzzled look on his face, "Okay then, I'll do what I can." However, he did not say anything about the request when he took me to the person in charge of the prayer house. Eventually, I dared to ask for myself. The person said, "That's fine. Pastor Cho is away right now. You can use the room for seven days."

The Lord did what He had said. My body was strengthened after that fasting. I have become busier at work but I have never been sick in bed since then. The Lord is alive, and He does what He tells us He will do.

CHAPTER 11

Proper use of prophecy and prophecy training

❧

Prophecy is just an ordinary affair

Soon after I was saved, I often attended the Keswick Convention held at the Yodobashi Church. I received many blessings through various messages at that convention, and, above all, the message brought by a Korean Pastor made a strong impression on me. He gave a testimony about dedicating his life to the Lord. In his testimony, he said that when he was a student walking along seashore, he heard the silent voice of God calling him to dedicate his life to Him. When I heard that, I was deeply impressed to learn that such a thing could happen, and at the same time I envied him. I felt that God spoke to him because he was special, but that God would not speak to me. However, I later learned that God speaks to anybody who has been saved, unless they firmly believe that God does not speak to them.

God speaking to us is not a special event, but an ordinary thing. Similarly, prophesying is also an ordinary affair. The First Corinthians 14:31 says, "For you can all prophesy one by one, that all may learn and all may be encouraged." It says that all of us, that is, all Christians can prophesy. Therefore, we can all prophesy. Of course, some may not want to prophesy; God will not force them to. However, anyone who is willing to prophesy can do so.

When I had just started to receive the charismatic gifts, I was at a meeting with several people. In the meeting we just sang praises to God and prayed in words and in tongues. But, one day, a woman suddenly said, "G... G...God is...l...l...light." The leader of the meeting was very glad to hear that and said, "A prophecy has been given." The leader also started to speak prophecies in a similar, hesitant manner. I was very glad to see this, but deep down I envied them. I wished that I could have prophesied also. At that time I did not know much about prophecy; everybody can prophesy.

Using prophecy in church-supervised meetings

When using prophecy, we should keep in mind that the gift of prophecy and its function belong to the church. Therefore, if we are going to prophesy, we must do it at a meeting held or permitted by the pastor of a church. When we use prophecy as a gift to the church, we are using the gift biblically and correctly; we are doing the Lord's will in the most suitable and safest way.

However, some people may say, "My pastor does not allow prophecy. What should I do?" In such a case, pray for your pastor, and if you are guided by the Lord, persuade him to accept prophecy. If persuasion does not work, continue to pray. For the Bible says, "Let all things be done decently and in order." (1 Corinthians 14:40) This verse particularly refers to tongues and prophecy. You should never disrupt the order of a church by prophesying at your own will.

Some people hold a private meeting to prophesy independently of their church, but I would advise not to do it.

The other day I watched a news program on TV. It reported that a car driven by a junior-high-school student was speeding and ploughed into a rice field. He was seriously injured and one elementary student in the car was killed. That junior-high-school student had stolen the car on the previous day, and was out driving with his friends. Of course, he did not have a driver's license and he had not been to driving school. He learned to drive the car just by looking at others driving. The end result was a serious accident.

I think that prophesying independently of a church is like driving a car without a license. I dread it may cause a serious accident. Even if serious accidents could be avoided, that way of using prophecy will result in nothing more than self-satisfaction because it is not the right way. For this reason, I advise that those who have used the gift of prophecy in the groups independent of churches be immediately brought under the authority of a church.

Obeying the leader appointed by the church

Once a meeting has been organized properly, keep in mind to obey the leader first of all.

One day, a person who was not a member of our church came to us and said, "I can't stop prophesying when prophecy comes to me." In other cases, some people who prophesy at meetings completely disregard the leader when he tries to bring them to order. These attitudes are unbiblical in two respects.

Firstly, they disturb the order in the church. Therefore, they are acting contrary to the Scripture: "Let all things be done decently and in order." Secondly, as 1 Corinthians 14:32 says, "And the spirits of the prophets are subject to the prophets," the spirits of the prophets, that is, the spirit of prophecy will obey the prophets. Therefore, if a person tries to stop prophesying, the spirit of prophecy will obey him. A person speaking a prophecy can stop speaking it. If someone cannot, such a prophecy is not from God, because it is contrary to the Bible. In that case, he mistakenly believes that he cannot stop prophesying, or an evil spirit is making him speak it.

In the meetings of prophecy, they need to be held under the supervision of a church and to be subject to the leader's authority. For this reason, I advise you not to prophesy when praying alone, and not to have meetings of prophecy without your pastor's permission.

We need training in prophecy

Let us seek prophecy in a church meeting as we all can prophesy. While praising and praying, turn our hearts and mind to God, and let us try to receive words from God. In most cases, prophecy comes into our heart. Speak the words that come into your heart.

Some might argue that we cannot tell if the words that come into our heart are really from God. They are right. Some words that come into our heart are from God, some from our own mind, and some even come from Satan. So, if you have just begun to prophesy, most of the words coming into your heart may be your own thoughts. However, keep speaking all the words that come into your heart as they come, because you need training. In the beginning, you may speak a true prophecy once out of every ten times or one hundred times. However, as you keep on training, you will be able to receive more words from God. Earnestly pursue prophecy and train yourself, for the Scripture says, "And desire spiritual gifts, but especially that you may prophesy." (1 Corinthians 14:1)

Our body has a lower specific gravity than water. Therefore, anybody can float in water. Anybody, a heavy-weight person, a light-weight person, a skinny person or a fat person, all will float in water. However, a person who cannot swim will sink in water. It is not that such a person has a greater specific gravity than an ordinary person. He has the same specific gravity as others but he sinks. Everybody sinks when they try to swim for the first time. However, after some swimming practice they will be able to float and swim in water.

When I went skiing for the first time in my life, I saw people skiing so smoothly and imagined that I would do the same. I thought that skiing would be easy. However, once I got on the snow with a pair of skis on, I started to slide down in the wrong direction. Soon I fell down, and was unable to stand up by myself with my legs tangled up with each other. However, after practicing a number of times I began to improve little by little. Everything requires training. Spiritual gifts are not an exception.

Growth through repetition

The pastor of the church where I ministered as an assistant pastor was originally from the evangelical stream. Around 1975 God started to lead him towards the charismatic activities. He did not immediately start praying for healing then, but first started studying about healing in the Bible and in other books on the subject. In the early stage, his prayer for healing worked only to the extent that his hands got warm when he prayed by laying hands on the sick. However, the pastor continued to pray for healing.

After a while, real healing started to happen. By the time I left the church to start church planting, outstanding healing had taken place through him. For example, the blind had their eyesight restored and people were healed of epilepsy and cancer. He is now one of the most well known vessels of God for healing.

He continued to pray repeatedly for healing in spite of the fact that healing did not take place. I can see that there was a process of training and practice until he achieved a result of real healing. This holds true for prophecy too. We all need training, except for specially gifted people who can prophesy excellently from the beginning. I started prophesying eight years ago, and my prophecy proficiency level has steadily improved along with training.

There are some forms of prophecy: an angel brings words, or a dream or a vision is given. However, prophecy mainly comes into our hearts. We should try to receive and speak the words coming from God into our hearts

Protection from danger through prophecy

In March 1997, I visited Sendai-city with my family for a ministry in the Tohoku District.

In the morning, when I was praying with my wife, I received a prophecy. The word, "Danger" came into my heart. The Lord told me about the danger of a traffic accident. I did not speak out that prophecy because my wife might have gotten panicky. However, in my heart I started to seriously pray for protection. When a warning is given, the Lord is leading us to pray about it. Through prayer we will be protected by God.

We went to Fukushima for a meeting, and after that we visited a church member's house. When we left the house, after having fellowship with him and his family, I sat in the seat next to the driver in the van. My eldest son came and sat on my lap. My second son, who saw that, got cross and would not come into the van. Just then, a car came towards us from the opposite direction. I shouted to him: "Look out. Move quick!" He ran to the sidewalk immediately, but the driver of our van got so upset that he steered to the right. The driver of the car in the oncoming lane naturally was going to steer his car to our right, but, on seeing our move, he became alarmed and veered back to our left. As a result, a collision was avoided, but our van crashed into the guardrail.

To be honest, I felt relieved, for the accident was over and was far less serious than I had expected. In my morning prayer time the Lord had given me the prophecy which told me about the danger of a traffic accident. He had enabled me to pray about it in advance. Prayer is a great blessing; He provided us with protection. This prophecy about the traffic accident came into my heart.

Jeremiah 20:9 says: "Then I said, 'I will not make mention of Him, nor speak anymore in His name.' But His word was in my heart like a burning fire shut up in my bones; I was weary of holding it back, and I could not." Jeremiah once made up his mind not to prophesy anymore because he was criticized for and laughed at the prophecies he had spoken. However, he could not keep prophecy contained in his heart as the words of prophecy flared up in his heart.

Prophecy is given in various forms, such as dreams, visions or words brought by an angel. The most common form, however, seems to be words coming into our heart.

Directions for pastoral ministry given through prophecy

Let us expect from God, and speak out the words when they are given. At the beginning, most of them may be your own thoughts. However, train yourself repeatedly, and do not disregard prophecy, for it is one of the ways which God uses to greatly bless us.

Let me tell you what happened when our team visited Texas. We were travelling by car all the way from Waco to Dallas. While we were praying and praising the Lord in the car, a prophecy was spoken. The prophecy said to the person driving the car, "Be prepared because you will become a pastor shortly." The person and all the others in the car wondered if it was true. No one thought that he was gifted in the area of pastoral ministry. Besides, the person himself had confessed that he would devote his whole life to church administration and driving, and that he was not called to be a pastor. God is wonderful; He knew the person better than we did, and even better than the person himself did. The Lord said that He had given him the gift of pastoral ministry. Eight years have passed since then. He is currently the pastor of a church in Kyushu District. Through him the Lord has started two more churches other than the one he pastors now. If the Lord had not spoken to us through prophecy, we, including himself, would have continued to believe till this day that he was not given the gift of pastoral ministry. He might have been walking in a direction that was not according to God's will. We will have much to lose by disregarding prophecy.

CHAPTER 12

True Prophets
and False Prophets

The reason for testing prophecy

Prophecy is neither fortune-telling nor foretelling itself. Although prophecy does include foretelling, it receives in trust all of God's Word, including teachings, directions, warnings etc. God gives His Word to prophets to speak.

I often ask a member of our church or mission staff to tell this to Brother A, or to tell that to Sister B. The message can be a greeting, an answer to a question or an instruction. Figuratively speaking, a staff member receives a message from me and speaks it (i.e. prophesies). You would understand me better by switching the relationship of myself and a staff member to that of God and a prophet. However, the words spoken by a prophet must be examined to see if he correctly spoke the words from God. In some cases, the prophet himself must be examined to check whether he is a true prophet or a false one.

Suppose I said to Brother A., "Ask Sister B. to bring me a glass of orange juice", but Brother A. heard me wrong and asked Sister B. to bring me a cup of tea. Suppose Brother A. was a prophet, he did not hear me correctly and gave the wrong instructions. Since this sort of thing could happen to any prophet, we have to test words spoken by prophets. In this case, the word the prophet spoke was wrong; he merely misheard the word or made a slip of the tongue. This is not a case in which a prophet himself should be tested. However, in other cases, we have to discern a false prophet.

One day, we received a phone call from a nearby bookshop. The shopkeeper asked my wife, who answered the phone, to come and pick up a copy of the book written by Daisaku Ikeda of Soka Gakkai as it was available. My wife could not believe what she heard. The shopkeeper said that the book had definitely been ordered under my own name. We still have not found out who ordered it. Nevertheless, someone using my name ordered something which I never asked for.

If applied to prophecy, the person who ordered the book is a false prophet. He spoke in my name and ordered the book even though I had not asked him to. Though false prophets are not sent by God, he goes in His name; though God does not speak to them, they prophesy. We should be careful of them.

Now, before discussing false prophets, let us see what kind of men or women are called prophets in the Bible.

What are prophets?

Prophets in the Old Testament and in the New Testament slightly differ in function although the word "prophet" similarly means "the one who receives the Word from God to speak" or "a person who speaks in His place."

In the Old Testament all of the people who prophesied were called prophets, people ranging from Isaiah and Jeremiah to the unknown prophets. Here is an example: "Then Saul sent messengers to take David. And when they saw the group of prophets prophesying, and Samuel standing as leader over them, the Spirit of God came upon the messengers of Saul, and they also prophesied." (1 Samuel 19:20) Apart from some exceptional situations, people who were called to be prophets were called prophets in Old Testament times.

In New Testament times, the definition of "prophet" has become a little more complicated. This is because the church started after the coming of the Holy Spirit at Pentecost. There were no churches in Old Testament times, but in New Testament times the church began and the gift of prophecy was positioned in part of the church, which is the body of Christ. Prophets should be understood in terms of their relationship to a church.

When reading the New Testament, we find that the word "prophet" is twofold. One appears in Ephesians 4:11: "And He Himself gave some to be apostles, some prophets, some evangelists, and some pastors and teachers". The word "prophet" in this verse does not mean just a person who prophesies. God gave the five offices to build up the churches: apostles, prophets, evangelists, pastors and teachers. They are chosen and appointed by God to be used to unify and build up the churches. They guide and instruct the churches with God-given authority.

The other appears in 1 Corinthians 14:31-32: "For you can all prophesy one by one, that all may learn and all may be encouraged. And the spirits of the prophets are subject to the prophets." This scripture says that the spirits of prophets obey prophets. Who are the prophets? They are all who prophesy as it says, "you can all prophesy one by one". In other words, people who prophesy are called "prophets". Verse 37 also says, "If anyone thinks himself to be a prophet or spiritual, let him acknowledge that the things which I write to you are the commandments of the Lord." The word "prophet" appears in this scripture as well, but it does not mean one of the "prophets" in the five offices. The word "prophets" in the five offices means a handful of people who are chosen and given authority over the churches by God, but the word here means all those people who prophesied in the church in Corinth. Soon after this, Paul gives them a caution about prophesying and speaking in tongues at the churches, saying, "Let all things be done decently and in order."(1 Corinthians 14:40)

To summarize, the word "prophet" is used in two ways in the New Testament. One means prophets specially appointed by God as one of the offices of the fivefold ministry, that is, the office of prophets; and the other generally means people who prophesy, such as those people who prophesied in the church in Corinth. Please know that this classification also applies in the case of false prophets.

What are false prophets?

False prophets share a common element. In Matthew 7, verses 15-16 say:

"Beware of false prophets, who come to you in sheep's clothing, but inwardly they are ravenous wolves. You will know them by their fruits. Do men gather grapes from thorn bushes or figs from thistles?"

Also, in Matthew 7, verses 22-23 say:

"Many will say to Me in that day, 'Lord, Lord, have we not prophesied in Your name, cast out demons in Your name, and done many wonders in Your name?' And then I will declare to them, 'I never knew you; depart from Me, you who practice lawlessness!'" These scriptures show that false prophets are not saved.

1 John 4, verses 1-3 also say:

"Beloved, do not believe every spirit, but test the spirits, whether they are of God; because many false prophets have gone out into the world. By this you know the Spirit of God: Every spirit that confesses that Jesus Christ has come in the flesh is of God, and every spirit that does not confess that Jesus Christ has come in the flesh is not of God. And this is the spirit of the Antichrist, which you have heard was coming, and is now already in the world."

These verses don't speak only about false prophets but describe a somewhat broader range than those, but naturally false prophets are included. These scriptures refer to the spirit that does not confess that Jesus has come in the flesh and to the spirit of the Antichrist.

Therefore, we can understand that false prophets are not saved.

Acts 13:6 gives a specific example of a false prophet: "Now when they had gone through the island to Paphos, they found a certain sorcerer, a false prophet, a Jew whose name was Bar-Jesus". In the following verses, they describe things which happened between Paul and this magician. Of course, this Bar-Jesus was not saved because he was a magician and Paul even called him "you son of the devil" (v 10). From what I have discussed, we can conclude that false prophets are not saved. Jesus said that they could be discerned by their fruit. They bear the fruits of hypocrisy and of sin because they are not saved. On reading the scripture about this fruit, some people argue that false prophets are Christians who are not sanctified enough due to some failings. However, the Scripture does not say so, but speaks of a more fundamental thing. In other words, their fruit will clearly prove that they are not saved.

My experience with a false prophet

Once, we, as a team of our church members went to attend a Christian conference in Waco, Texas. During the several days of the conference session, the speakers from various countries, but mainly from the United States gave messages; we had a wonderful time of worship and heard a number of prophecies spoken out.

In the conference there was an African evangelist who sang solo praise songs. During the first meeting early next morning, after a message we had a time of prayer. All of the attendees started praying; some of them were kneeling down, some were walking around, and some others came forward onto the stage to pray. When we had been praying for a while, an African in ragged clothes came in. He was carrying a bucket full of filth, and started to scatter the filth on the stage. While he was doing this, he started to prophesy in a loud voice; he spoke words full of hate and spoke out curses one after another. When this happened, some female participants panicked. Some people tried to stop him, but his violence intimidated them. Finally, five or six men forced him outside. We could not believe that he was a Christian. Later, we were surprised to find out that he was the evangelist from Africa who had sung praise songs the day before. His behavior could be judged in various ways, but I don't think that he had been saved at all. I sensed the opposite fruit in him. It was not that he did not have enough of the fruits of the Holy Spirit; he did what a Christian would never do. I heard that he was angry because he had been given few ministry opportunities during the conference.

Just as there are true prophets, there are also false prophets. We have to discern false prophets because they try to confuse and destroy meetings and churches, especially in the area of teaching and church order. In some cases, they even act violently. False prophets have never accepted Jesus Christ and the true gospel. They pretend to be angels of light even though they are not obeying God. We should be wary of them. They sneak into churches and even do signs and wonders. Since the work of prophecy is wonderful, Satan tries to make good use of it. We need to discern false prophets and false workers.

Be ready for the third day

True prophets speak wonderful prophecies. Of course, any prophecy must be examined, but through them God's will is revealed to us and His glory is manifested.

For a while after "The Water Flowing from the Sanctuary Mission" started, a family kindly let us use a room of their rented house for the mission office. However, the Lord began to speak through prophets about the office location. He told us to move the office. He said further specifically that He had prepared an office on the third floor of a building several minutes on foot from Kokubunji Station.

However, we did not have enough faith to believe that prophecy. At that time, it cost ten million yen to rent an office in a building near the station. Though we were praying for the money, we did not think that we would be given such a large amount of money. At that time, a problem arose. The family providing us with mission office space had to move out of their house within several weeks.

We were perturbed, because we did not have any place to move to and we did not have any money. We started to pray more earnestly about it.

At that time we were shown through the Word: "And he said to the people, 'Be ready for the third day.'" (Exodus 19:15) As it was given very clearly, I told my wife about it, and we said to each other that the third day would fall on Sunday or Monday.

On Monday evening, which was the third day, I was having a meeting with several staff members, when the man in charge of accounting suddenly said, "I've just remembered. We received a donation at noon." A donation of ten million yen had been transferred to our account.

The Lord provided us with the necessary money for the mission office. We lacked in faith but the Lord is almighty. He provided us with the necessary money at the right time. After this, however, we had another problem. We started to look for the office in an area considerably larger than what had been prophesied. We were afraid we would not be able to find an office within several minutes' walk from Kokubunji Station, as prophesied. However, one building owner after another refused to let an office to us because we were a Christian organization. After being refused about twenty times, we received a reply saying that two offices were available. We moved into one of them in April 1991. This office is on the third floor of a building several minutes' walk from Kokubunji Station. It's exactly as it was spoken through the prophecy. God is alive; we moved into the place He had prepared for us.

Six years have passed since then. Now the place has become too small for us, and we are praying for a move. However, this place is surely the one God gave us. We have received many blessings there. What God does is perfect. We should not disregard His Word.

CHAPTER 13

Prophecies not fulfilled although they are from God

❧

W hen I first started to plant a church, I was living
with my co-worker. One day, a man who said
that he was a fire-station employee came to sell us a
fire extinguisher. He told us about fire precautions and
that every household was required to buy a fire extinguisher by law. My co-worker was almost deceived,
but I was not because I had replaced old fire extinguishers as a part-time job when I was a student. When
I said that nobody was required to buy it by law, the
man left us saying, "If this house is burnt down, it's
your responsibility." Later, the fire station distributed a
warning in that area about people fraudulently selling
fire extinguishers.

That man was a con man pretending to be a fire
station employee. I think he was cunning. Most people
would be deceived if a person pretending to be a fire
station employee falsely tells them that the law requires
them to buy a fire extinguisher as a precaution against

fire. Con men are cunning. Satan, however, is much more cunning; he pretends to be an angel of light to deceive people. He often imitates God's word to tell us what he wants. He also imitates God's works.

Satan is a cunning con man

I have seen people praying in the street with their hands spread over others. It is healing by evil spirits. They imitate the healing of God.

Also, Shoko Asahara of the Aum religious cult prophesied and declared about Armageddon. At the same time, strangely enough, he worshipped Shiva of Hinduism. The fact that he prophesied and warned about Armageddon makes us wonder if he is like a Christian. Of course, what he was saying was full of nonsense and deception, far from what the Bible says. He was obviously imitating things of God.

One of the assertions of the New Age Movement is positive thinking. This is an imitation of walking by faith and confession of faith in Christianity although it differs from them in that it does not rely on God. Such examples are countless. Satan deceives people by imitations. Many people are deceived by such imitations. Satan is a cunning con man.

These imitation works of Satan confuse some people about what a real thing of God is. For example, as Mark 16:18 says, "they will lay hands on the sick, and they will recover," praying and laying hands on the sick looks just the same as what new religion groups are doing. And so, when some people find a church where they pray for healing, they think it is the same as what the new religious groups are doing. Also, when Christians talk about Armageddon or prophecy from the Bible, some people think that these Christians are, after all, the same as Aum believers who claim similar things.

Also, "confession of faith in God" and "walking by faith" sound similar to the positive thinking of the New Age Movement. Therefore, some people hear those terms and say, "Oh, it's New Age."

Satan is an imitator; when people see imitations of Satan first, and then genuine works of God, they often get confused.

Seeing imitations

In 1996, when I went to the Amazon, I boarded a boat down the river, which looked like a large lake to me, and began to see an island. I got off the boat on the island where a souvenir shop was, and saw a boy with a stuffed toy sloth in his arms coming up to me. Wondering if he came to sell that toy to me, I reached out to touch it; I was surprised to see it suddenly move before touching it. It was not a stuffed toy, but a real sloth that looked just like a stuffed toy. I had seen stuffed toys in many places and, as a result, I mistook the real animal for a stuffed one (i.e. imitation).

A similar thing often occurs in Christian churches. People who often see imitations mistake the genuine thing for an imitation: for example, "Healing is strange because new religion groups do it," "Aum talks about Armageddon and prophesies so these must be cult things," "Works by spiritual gifts are of the occult,"

"Confession of faith is the positive thinking of the New Age Movement," etc. If we try to judge the genuine through our experiences with imitations, we are mislead and confused.

Seeing genuine things

Then, what is the solution to the problem of being confused by imitations? I have heard of the best way to recognize counterfeit bills. If you just think about it for a moment, you would imagine that the best way would be to scrutinize the counterfeit bills keenly, but that's not the case. Scrutinizing the counterfeit bills only confuses you because a new kind of counterfeit bill comes out in sequence.

What is the best solution then? It is to handle genuine bills. It is said that people who have been handling the genuine thing and have known the feel of it can recognize counterfeits easily.

What are genuine things to us? They are God and the Bible. We should keep in contact with God, and examine and discern things through God's word. Then we can see what things are genuine and what the truth is. In the Bible we can read about healing by laying hands on the sick, Armageddon, walking by faith through positive confession, tongues and prophecy. We must not lose the real things by seeing some false ones.

Prophecy of judgment

When we study prophecy, we come across the interesting fact: some prophecies are not fulfilled even though they seem to be definitely from God. Of course, unfulfilled prophecies are usually considered wrong ones. However, there are some cases where prophecies are not fulfilled even though they are not wrong (i.e. they were given by God).

Let's look at some examples in this chapter. The book of Jonah tells us the story of the prophet Jonah. God ordered him to go to Nineveh, the capital of Assyria, to prophesy there, but he disobeyed and fled. However, as God's hand was upon him, he could not escape, and was swallowed up by a large fish. He repented and was rescued by God miraculously from the fish's belly. He rose up again as a prophet of the Lord and prophesied in Nineveh.

Jonah 3:4 says, "And Jonah began to enter the city on the first day's walk. Then he cried out and said, 'Yet forty days, and Nineveh shall be overthrown!'" The prophecy said that Nineveh would be destroyed in forty days. However, Jonah 3:10 says, "Then God saw their works, that they turned from their evil way; and God relented from the disaster that He had said He would bring upon them, and He did not do it." God "relented" from the disaster and He did not send it. In this case the prophecy was not fulfilled even though it was certainly from God. Even prophecies truly spoken by God are not fulfilled in some cases.

There are three types of prophecies that are not fulfilled even though they are given by God. The first one is prophecy about judgment, as described in the book of Jonah. The Lord gives a prophecy of judgment to people who have sinned. Most of the prophecies in Old Testament times were about judgment. However, when a prophecy is given along with a condition such as, "if you repent wholeheartedly," or even if such a condition is not attached, disaster will not always be brought if people repent like the people of Nineveh. This is because God can change His mind if people repent.

Prophecy of warning

The second type is a prophecy of warning. Jonah's prophecy was a warning as well as a judgment. Some warnings are given people so that they can prepare against them as in the case of the warning Joseph interpreted to get people to prepare for the coming famine. Some other warnings are given so that people can avoid disaster if they repent or pray about it, as found in the book of Jonah.

I once visited the U.S. with a team of church members to attend Christian camp meetings at Los Angeles and Waco. We had to drive a rent-a-car for three hours to get to Waco from Dallas Airport. Before this trip to the U.S., some prophecies were given; one of them said, "The cassette player of Brother A.'s and Sister B.'s will be stolen in Dallas. So pray about it." In our schedule we were going to stop by in Dallas only for a short time to use its airport on our way to and from Waco.

On hearing this prophecy, Brother A. prayed about it a little and then forgot about it. However, Sister B. was praying seriously and diligently. The problem really happened in Dallas. Brother A.'s cassette player was stolen, but Sister B.'s was not. This incident taught us the importance of prayer. The prophecy was not fulfilled for the person who prayed about it.

When prophecy of this type is spoken, we should repent in some cases and should pray about it in other cases. Our repentance or prayer will often stop the fore-warned problem from happening, or will protect us from it even it does not stop it.

One day, a prophecy was given about a Christian brother. It said that he would lose his life in an earthquake. We did not tell him about the prophecy, but we could not leave it as it was, either. We started to pray for him and to intercede that his life would be protected. Soon afterwards, he moved from Tokyo to Kobe.

One night, near the end of 1994, my wife suddenly woke me up at midnight. She told me that she had seen a great crowd of dead people. My wife and I were convinced that something was going to happen. In January the following year, a great earthquake hit the Hanshin area. The area in Kobe where the brother moved to was the most heavily hit. We looked for his name in the death toll columns of the newspaper, but fortunately we could not find his name. Later, we were informed of his safety. We heard that he said that he had been given God's special protection.

When we receive a warning prophecy, we need to pray about it because it is through prayer that the Lord may help us or protect us. From my experience, the percentage of His responding to our prayers seems to be quite high.

Prophecy about calling

The third one is prophecy about mission work, mission tasks and future calling. As for this type of prophecy, I have seen the prophecies spoken to some people fulfilled exactly, and the prophecies spoken to other people unfulfilled even though those prophecies seemed to be correct.

Why do they have different results? The person who receives a calling from God for mission work and task naturally has to obey God in order for it to be fulfilled. Therefore, with some special exceptions, we should consider that a prophecy about calling or the like contains the condition that the person given the prophecy must obey. In most cases, prophecies of this type are fulfilled when we obey God, but remain unfulfilled when we do not obey Him.

In April 1984, when we started to plant a church in Tokyo, the Lord told us to name our church "Center". He also told us that this church would play the role of a center in various aspects. This was certainly God's calling, for our church has been functioning as the center in setting up new churches, promoting overseas missions and running a seminary.

Regarding church planting in particular, the Lord told us through prophecy to set up churches throughout Japan. Our first daughter church was planted in Nagasaki. To be honest, I was upset when Pastor Kihara, who now ministers at the church in Nagasaki, came and said to me, "The Lord has shown me that I am to go to Nagasaki."

It was true that God was telling me to plant churches

in various locations, but I thought it was a long time in the future. On top of that, Pastor Kihara was playing an important role in our church in Tokyo. Besides, if he went to Nagasaki, the church would have to support him. I thought that planting a church in Nagasaki would be just a waste and would be of no benefit at all. However, when I prayed, the Lord said to me, "This is my plan." Finally, I reluctantly sent Pastor Kihara and his family off to Nagasaki.

After Pastor Kihara and his family went to Nagasaki, nobody attended his church for a year. Pastor Kihara later told me that he had been disappointed many times and had thought of coming back to Tokyo. However, he stayed in the place of God's will for him. About ten years have passed since then. Our daughter churches in the Kyushu area currently number around twenty; many churches were birthed from the church in Nagasaki.

At the moment, there are 82 churches throughout Japan under the covering of the Lord's Cross Christian Center. The calling God has given to us is being fulfilled. However, if I had not accepted the Lord's will, even reluctantly, or if Pastor Kihara had not left for Nagasaki in obedience to the Lord, or if he had come back to Tokyo, forsaking His will because of the difficulties, the calling to plant churches would not have been fulfilled. In most cases, the calling is fulfilled when we obey the Lord.

Some prophecies, even though they are from God, may not be fulfilled. Therefore, let's handle them carefully.

CHAPTER 14

Prophecy is a sword given by the Holy Spirit

❧

Prophecy is a weapon for spiritual warfare

Recently an increasing number of churches have begun to deal with spiritual warfare. They have opened their eyes to Satan's various activities; with that awareness, the warfare against those activities has been in the spotlight. In this spiritual warfare, prophecy is a powerful weapon.

In Ephesians 6:10 and onwards the Bible talks about spiritual warfare. Verse 17 says, "And takes the helmet of salvation, and the sword of the Spirit, which is the word of God." Other verses describe defensive armor, but verse 17 tells us about a sword, an offensive weapon. God's word is a sword to cut down the enemy. Here, God's word primarily means the Bible, the infallible word of God; the word in the Bible is a sword to cut down Satan. Secondly, it means the word of God spoken through prophecy. However, the prophecies that are not from God after tested should be excluded, but the correct words through prophecy are the word of God. This word, as a sword given by the Holy Spirit, will defeat and overpower the enemy. For spiritual warfare, we have been given this sword, the word through prophecy, in addition to the Bible.

Let us see how prophecy cuts away at Satan's activities or, in a broader sense, problems caused by him by discussing it from three different viewpoints.

Prophecy foretells the enemy's moves

Firstly, prophecy foretells the moves of the enemy; in a broader sense, it foretells the future problems. The walks of Christians and churches are ceaselessly under attack from Satan; neither Christians nor churches are free from problems in their walk. God will tell us through prophecy the moves of Satan and what problems to expect.

We can see an interesting description in 2 Kings 6:8-12:

"Now the king of Syria was making war against Israel; and he consulted with his servants, saying, 'My camp will be in such and such a place.' And the man of God sent to the king of Israel, saying, 'Beware that you do not pass this place, for the Syrians are coming down there.' Then the king of Israel sent someone to the place of which the man of God had told him. Thus he warned him, and he was watchful there, not just once or twice. Therefore the heart of the king of Syria was greatly troubled by this thing; and he called his servants and said to them, 'Will you not show me which of us is for the king of Israel?' And one of his servants said, 'None, my lord, O king; but Elisha, the prophet who is in Israel, tells the king of Israel the words that you speak in your bedroom.'"

This passage says that a prophet, Elisha, is telling the king of Israel the enemy's moves. This prophet helped Israel to know the enemy's move in advance which enabled them to protect themselves and defeat the enemy. Through prophecy, we can know Satan's moves and what problems to anticipate.

Prophecy plays the role of watchman

Prophecy has the role of watchman. Our judgment, based on what our eyes see and what our ears hear, is limited, but the Lord knows everything. We do not know what will happen in the future but He does. Through prophecy He tells us about future events and helps us prepared for them.

In the Philippines we had a three-day crusade. On the day of highest attendance, there was a special gathering of about 2500 people. At that time a prophecy was given to us, saying that the meeting would be blessed but that you would be under a strong spiritual attack. It also said that someone would fall ill after the meeting, caused by the spiritual attack.

Through prophecy God told us about it in advance, but we did not pay much attention to it and did not pray about it enough. The meeting was blessed, but immediately after it a female team member started to run a temperature. By the time we got back to our lodging house, she was having a high fever. We prayed for her but she did not get any better.

We decided to keep her in bed and see how she would be the next day. She seemed to have caught cold and did not improve at all the next day. Prayers and medicine did not help her condition. We had never had this kind of trouble in our previous teams; some members had got sick, but they had recovered quickly without having to stay so long in bed.

On the following morning she still had a high temperature. We finally decided to take her to hospital, but one thing bothered me. It was the prophecy saying that someone would fall ill after the meetings due to spiritual attack. I suspected that her illness might have been caused by evil spirits, and decided to do spiritual warfare before taking her to hospital.

I started praying with several team members for a spiritual solution. There was a nurse in our group. She had seen many people healed during the meetings, but she was thinking that she had not witnessed any evidence of healing. She had told others that she had wanted to see clear evidence of healing before her eyes. We had that nurse take the patient's temperature and then started praying. When we started to treat the spiritual problem, the temperature suddenly began to go down. Ten minutes later I got the nurse to take the temperature again. "Oh, my!," she exclaimed. She saw God's healing before her eyes. God had lowered her temperature to normal ten minutes later. That illness was caused by evil spirits as the prophecy had said. When we took necessary action against the evil spirits, the temperature dropped in ten minutes.

Through prophecy the Lord tells us about Satan's

135

moves. Satan tries to move invisibly and without being noticed but the Lord knows everything. He warns us through prophecy and tells us what to do.

Prophecy cuts away deception

Secondly, prophecy cuts away deception. Satan is a deceiver. Our sins also deceive us. Under such conditions we are apt to let go of God's words, be misled into a wrong direction and get off track. God, through prophecy, exposes those deceptions and misleading.

Overseas missions were first shown to us as our calling through the Word, and then through prophecy. We were filled with hope and enthusiasm for going out into the whole world. However, even then we were thinking that how this would be possible. We started to prepare for it diligently. As years passed by with nothing happening, we were filled with a negative thought that such preparation would come to nothing, or that the way to overseas missions would never be opened. Such strong deception came in because of Satan's deception and because of our sinful nature.

However, prophecy cut away those thoughts. It continued to speak to us about overseas missions and encouraged us to continue preparing for them. Those words of prophecy released us from our negative thinking and from deceptive thoughts.

It was quite natural for us to think that we had been dreaming about world missions, or had been acting on a deceptive vision, for none of us had any experience in overseas missions, none of us could speak English, none of us had been abroad and none of us knew how to participate in overseas missions. But God, with words of prophecy, the spiritual sword, cut away our human ideas, unbelief, deceptive thoughts, etc. every time they surfaced.

God told us that He would plant many churches throughout Japan. But, how often we thought it was impossible! We were easily deceived by Satan. However, God cut away Satan's deception, our human thoughts and unbelieving thinking, using the word of prophecy as a spiritual sword.

We need the Word of God, a spiritual sword, to live a Christian life filled with blessings towards its end and to accomplish God's given task. The Bible, of course, plays the major role for that, but God has provided us with the word of prophecy as a spiritual sword.

God provides the function of prophecy, as well as the Word of the Bible, for us to walk His way without being deceived or led astray. By using this gift of prophecy, we are armed with a powerful weapon against Satan's attempts to deceive and mislead us, and against our human thinking.

Prophecy is effective in spiritual warfare

Thirdly, prophecy is effective in direct warfare against the evil spirits. Through prophecy, the Lord gives us directions of spiritual warfare and leads us to do it.

Once, when our church members and I visited a Christian's house in a rural area, a prophecy was given at a prayer meeting there, telling us to bind a strong man of the area. The prophecy went on to say specifically that it was the spirit of a Shinto shrine on a hilltop overlooking the area, and that the *torii* gate of the shrine was not painted red but was made of stone and had a sacred straw rope stretched between its pillars. The person in the Christian home told us that he did not know if the *torii* gate was made of red stone or white one, but there certainly was such a shrine.

The shrine, as the prophecy had said, was on a hilltop and was the worship center of the area; it was dedicated to the feudal lord who once governed the area, for his divine protection. We actually went there on the hilltop, and found the shrine, just the same as the prophet told us he had seen in the vision. What is more, the *torii* gate was not painted red, but was made of white stone; it had a sacred straw rope stretched between its pillars. We prayed and bound the evil spirit there.

Through prophecy God shows us about spiritual warfare and He leads us to wage spiritual warfare. We recently waged spiritual warfare at Mount Osore in Aomori Prefecture, Kotohira Shrine, known as Konpira in the Shikoku District, and Izumo shrine in the Chugoku District.

As a matter of fact, God had told us to do spiritual warfare at those places nearly ten years before. However, we had been hesitant about it because of our lack of confidence. However, for those ten years we had seen little progress in our mission work in the Tohoku District where Mt. Osore is, the Shikoku District where Konpira is and the Chugoku District where Izumo shrine is. Now, I think that the lack of progress in mission work in those districts may have had something to do with the fact that we had not waged spiritual warfare there.

In spiritual warfare, we usually pray, praise the Lord, declare the Lord's victory, bind evil spirits, give the evil spirits a command, speak the Word of God, which is the sword of the Spirit, and prophesy. Like the Words of the Bible, prophecy is also the sword of the Spirit that directly strikes Satan. Every time we prophesy, we strike Satan with the sword. Prophecy is one of the weapons of spiritual warfare; it is extremely powerful against Satan. God's work through prophecy is wonderful; prophecy can be used in various aspects. We should not disregard this spiritual gift.

The way to Indonesia

At the beginning of 1997 there was a prophecy which said, "I will lead you to Indonesia." Actually, thirty years ago, I had dedicated myself to God for mission work in Indonesia. I was not called as a long-term missionary, but it had been thirty years since I had been called to Indonesia.

Overseas mission work had begun and expanded, with openings to Asia, North America, Europe, Africa and South America. Strangely the way to Indonesia had remained closed. I had tried to visit the country twice in the past, but was stopped by the Lord both times. The Lord told me through the Bible: "Therefore we wanted to come to you—even I, Paul, time and again—but Satan hindered us." (1 Thessalonians 2:18)

In July 1997, the way to Indonesia was suddenly opened to us even though we had had no opportunities before. The way to ministry was opened to us just as the prophecy had said. We were given an opportunity to minister at the largest church in the country, a church of 40,000 members, and at another church where five Christians, including the pastor and his wife, were martyred in October 1996. The way was opened not only to the country, but to the churches that seemed most important to us. God's work is excellent.

As I was standing in front of a large audience praising the Lord, just before delivering the first message in that country, I thought to myself: "I have finally got to Indonesia." The call and dedication to Indonesian missions thirty years ago, right after I got saved, was fulfilled at last just as the prophecy had said. The Lord is faithful; He fulfils what he has spoken without fail.

We should never abandon what God has shown us even though we forget it at times. As a tree bears fruit when the time comes, His plan will be fulfilled in His time.

That morning, from the scriptural passage for devotions for that day, I received the word: "It is done!" (Revelation 21: 6)

CHAPTER 15

God's word is fulfilled in His time

❧

Prophecy is fulfilled in His time

"So shall My word be that goes forth from My mouth; It shall not return to Me void, But it shall accomplish what I please, And it shall prosper in the thing for which I sent it." (Isaiah 55:11)

God is alive and He speaks to us; He comforts us, encourages us, leads us to repentance, and gives us directions and promises. All of God's words are right and will be fulfilled as spoken. If there is a condition attached with some of His words, they will be fulfilled by meeting the condition; or some of His words without conditions will be fulfilled unconditionally. His word will never change. We experience His faithfulness through His word.

However, there is the time God appointed for His word to be fulfilled. Most of us are too impatient to wait for His time, or we are likely to presume that the time will come much earlier than it actually does.

God will fulfill His word without fail, but only in His time. In most cases, we feel that it takes too long. In some cases, the Word is fulfilled long after we were first shown it, or after we had already forgotten it because it seemed to take so long.

Noah's case

It is said to have been one hundred years from the time when God said to Noah, "Build an ark because a flood is coming," until the time when it actually started to rain to have floods. Genesis 5:32 says, "And Noah was five hundred years old, and Noah begot Shem, Ham, and Japheth." Genesis 6:10, three verses before the one that describes God's order to Noah to build the ark, also says, "And Noah begot three sons: Shem, Ham, and Japheth." These scriptures seem to indicate the time of God's order; Noah heard God's voice when he was five hundred years old.

Genesis 7:6 describes the time of the flood, saying "Noah was six hundred years old when the floodwaters were on the earth." Therefore, God's timing came one hundred years after Noah had started building the ark at God's order. Of course, God's timing is the best, but it makes us wonder how late His timing is because we are not patient enough to wait for it.

However, Noah, in the desert of the Middle East where the rainfall was quite rare, went on to build an ark more than 100 meters in length, a huge ship at that time. Noah must have doubted at times; he might have thought how stupid it was of him to build a ship in the desert; or he might have doubted if God had really spoken to him about that or if he was following the wrong track. We are always tested before God's word is fulfilled. Finally the time of God had come; Genesis 7:11 says, "In the six hundredth year of Noah's life, in the second month, the seventeenth day of the month, on that day all the fountains of the great deep were broken up, and the windows of heaven were opened." There is something dynamic when God's word is fulfilled; He fulfills His word in His time.

God told Abraham that He would give the land of Canaan to his descendants; however, it took around six hundred years that this promise of God was fulfilled. Although, before that, Abraham bought a small burial site in Canaan, His promise was truly accomplished after around six hundred years.

Joseph's case

God showed Joseph some future events in his dream, and it took twenty-one years that they were realized (Genesis 42:8). We should not decide that what God showed us is not from Him just because it was not fulfilled soon, and neither should we stop following Him with a sense of mistrust. If what was shown to us is really from the Lord, it will be fulfilled without fail in His time; however, if we stop obeying God, it will not be fulfilled.

What's more, as for Noah and Joseph, what God told them seemed unlikely to happen.

In Joseph's case, his destiny headed in the opposite direction to what he had been shown. Joseph was shown in his dream that he would be promoted to a position where his parents and brothers would bow down before him. However, what actually happened to him soon after the dream was quite different. He was envied by his brothers because of his dream, and was sold as a slave. What actually happened to him was the opposite to being promoted.

On top of that, a few years later something worse happened, and he was finally thrown into prison on a false charge. Given this situation, his promotion is impossible. He was not only sold to Egypt as a slave, but was also imprisoned as a criminal. His life went on in a completely different direction from what God had showed him in his dream. As the time went by, the dream seemed increasingly impossible to come true. Psalm 105:19 says, "Until the time that his word came to pass, the word of the Lord tested him." Joseph was tested.

We, too, are often tested after God shows us something. God tests us to see if we really trust in Him. As in the case of Joseph, the opposite of what was shown us may repeatedly happen to us. Like Joseph, we may be placed in a situation where the fulfillment of what was shown seems impossible. God permits us trials. However, the Lord is faithful, and His word will be fulfilled in His time.

The Lord raised Joseph from a slave to the position of governor at the age of 30. The Lord performed this work by giving Joseph the interpretation of the king of Egypt's dream. At the age of 38, Joseph's brothers came to Joseph in Egypt and bowed down before him. This happened twenty-one years after

God had shown this to him in the dream, when he was only seventeen years old. God fulfilled what He said He would do; He does not tell lies. His word will never return in vain.

Prophecy is one of the important ways that God uses to speak to us. When a prophecy really comes from Him, it will always be fulfilled. Therefore, we should not let go of it easily, even though it does not come true as soon as we would like. Prophecy, if it is from the Lord, will always be fulfilled when the conditions are met if it is conditional; or it will be fulfilled unconditionally if no condition is attached.

Orphanage ministry revealed

In the early 1970s, God told me about orphanage work. Through George Mueller's book I learned about obeying the voice of God, and at the same time God spoke deeply into my heart about orphanage work. I prayed several times in those days: "Let me work for an orphanage."

Later, when prophecy started being spoken in our church in the mid 1980s, God started to speak more specifically about orphanages. The prophecy said that He would establish orphanages in various countries around the world. I thought that it was impossible when I first heard this word, but I kept it in mind just the same.

A little while later, God started the work by using us to help and support an orphanage in Romania. Our overseas mission office became the contact for donations for the orphanage construction and its work there. We have already sent about twenty million yen in donations, and three missionaries have been also sent from our church to work there.

Later we started to send donations regularly to an orphanage in India, and we are now supporting some orphanages in Kenya and Cambodia. Amazingly, many of God's vessels we were in a cooperative relationship with had been involved in orphanage work. We did not make any move ourselves to become involved with orphanages. It just happened naturally and we then began to work cooperatively with them. However, the Lord had told us that we would run orphanages ourselves.

In 1997, God specifically opened the way; we sent a lady missionary to Cambodia to establish an orphanage of our own. We had already acquired some know-how through several years of working cooperatively with orphanages. God's plans are perfect.

We have also been led to start an orphanage in the Philippines. We already have two children to take care of, and we are now waiting for the orphanage to be government-approved. We are also planning to establish an orphanage in Vietnam.

Our former prayers are now being answered and what God told us are now being fulfilled. More than ten years have passed since that specific prophecy was given. What we thought was totally impossible is now being easily achieved by the Lord; His time has come.

We should not abandon the way the Lord shows us even when the fulfillment of what He has told us seems delayed or impossible. What He has told us will be fulfilled in His time. What previously seemed impossible will be achieved miraculously or in a way that looks quite natural when it happens in His time.

God's plan for establishing churches and how that was fulfilled

Since God told us to start churches in Nagasaki and Hokkaido, we started them. God further told us that these churches would birth many churches. However, nobody attended either of them for a long time even though they were started at different times. As a result, the pastor sent to Nagasaki later told me that he went to the airport and nearly fled from that city; the pastor sent to Hokkaido once wanted to run away to a place where nobody knew him.

For the first year, no one attended those two churches even though they were given promises, and even though God Himself had started them. The pastors were tested in such a situation that seemed completely opposite to what the Lord had spoken. However, the Lord is faithful, and He does His work in His time. He started His work in Nagasaki and Hokkaido when it seemed impossible to see some work there. As of 1997, there are about twenty churches in the Kyushu District, with Nagasaki Church as the original church. In the Hokkaido District there are about ten churches, followed by the planting of the Hokkaido Church in Otaru.

We should never abandon the promise God has given to us and the way He has shown us to walk in. If the pastors had given up along the way and fled, God's work would not have taken place, and they would have ended up being the losers. However, when we keep on walking His way, we will see His works.

Specifying the fulfillment time of prophecy

We should keep walking His way patiently until the end. However, some people want to decide a time; we need to be careful of this because such thoughts often come from the flesh, and they can easily be used by Satan to deceive us.

This holds true for prophecy. We must be careful about prophecies which specify a period, a month or a day. In most cases, we tend to speak those kinds of prophecies out of our own minds, or we are being deceived by Satan. Hananiah the prophet prophesied, "Thus says the Lord: 'Even so I will break the yoke of Nebuchadnezzar king of Babylon from the neck of all nations within the space of two full years.'" This prophecy was wrong, and Hananiah was judged by God (Jeremiah 28:11). Hananiah spoke out of his own mind.

A prophecy specifying a period, a year, a month or a day of the month very often reflects prophet's human thoughts. If such a prophecy is spoken and you do not know if it is right or wrong, my advice is that you just keep it in mind. Do not be too concerned about it and do not let it influence you, otherwise it often brings bad results. We should handle such a prophecy with wisdom.

Nevertheless, specifying the fulfillment time of prophecy is a subtle issue; we should be very careful about it. However, prophecy is a wonderful blessing.

We should never disregard prophecies coming from God. When we hold on to them firmly, we will see His glory.

God told us about new relationships

On August 17, 1997, we invited Pastor Valnice Milhomens, a well-known T.V. evangelist in Brazil, to come and minister at our church. She is one of the most powerfully used vessels of the Lord in Brazil. In her message she delivered the Lord's words with the boldness that I did not expect from a woman.

It was through prophecy that we invited Pastor Valnice. A staff member of our church, who is a Japanese Brazilian, visited his country for three weeks and came back to Japan on August 6, 1997. Before his return a prophecy was spoken about him. It said that he would enable us to form relationships with God's vessels in Portuguese-speaking countries (including Brazil). When he contacted me, saying that one of God's vessels from Brazil wanted to meet me, I immediately knew that it was from the Lord. That is because the Lord had told me about that through prophecy in my early morning prayer time that day. The church staff member told me that Pastor Valnice did not know him, but he happened to board the same flight as hers on his way back to Japan. In the course of their conversation, she heard about our church; she felt the Lord's leading and contacted me so she could see me.

When we met and talked, I was surprised to learn that the Lord had arranged this meeting in His wonderful way. So, we entered into a cooperative relationship at our first meeting. She offered to cooperate fully with us in our work in Brazil, and requested that we make a T.V. appearance. Also, the relationships with two other world-famous vessels of God, which had been prophesied, opened up through her.

We should never disregard prophecy as the Lord does many of His works through it. His works are wonderful.

CHAPTER 16

The Cross we have to bear when we use the spiritual gift of prophecy

❦

Desire earnestly to prophesy

The First Corinthians 14:1 says, "Pursue love, and desire spiritual gifts, but especially that you may prophesy." This Scripture tells us about different aspects of prophecy. It first mentions love and then spiritual gifts. Love is most important, but spiritual gifts are also important. The Lord tells us to desire spiritual gifts, particularly to earnestly desire to prophesy. The reason He says so is that He is going to use this spiritual gift. Each spiritual gift, including prophecy, has its own special function; specific areas of the Lord's work will not be achieved unless we use prophecy and the other spiritual gifts.

In the Warring States period in Japan, there was an important battle called the battle of Nagashino. The outcome of this battle gave Nobunaga Oda the upper

hand. Katsuyori Takeda, a feudal lord in the powerful country of Kai, led his army against the combined armies of Oda and Tokugawa at a place called
Nagashino. Takeda's cavalrymen were unbeatable and
his soldiers were probably superior to those of Oda and
Tokugawa. However, the combined armies of Oda and
Tokugawa won an overwhelming victory. Why? It was
because they used guns. Nobunaga Oda divided his
gunners into three bands so that each band could take
turns shooting, one after the other. While one group
was shooting, two other groups were loading their
guns. That way there were no intervals between the
firing. Takeda's cavalry, which was charging unceas-
ingly, was mowed down by the guns. The army of
Oda and Tokugawa had an overwhelming victory. The
cause of the victory was guns. If they had not used
guns effectively, they would almost certainly have
been defeated.

The choice of the weapon decides victory or defeat.
Spiritual gifts are weapons the Lord has provided for
us, and prophecy is one of them. The Lord's works
are demonstrated to us abundantly when we use the
weapons He provides us with. When we use the Lord's
weapons, we can overwhelm the enemy. We should
fully use spiritual gifts, particularly prophecy.

The importance of prophecy from a Biblical viewpoint

The Scriptures that include the word 'prophecy'
appear no fewer than 198 times in the New Testament
alone. In the Early Church, prophecy was used

effectively. Even if we take just some of the Scriptures including the word 'prophecy' in the New Testament, we will see how prophecy played a major role in the church:

"Therefore, brethren, desire earnestly to prophesy, and do not forbid to speak with tongues." (1 Corinthians 14:39); "Do not despise prophecies." (1 Thessalonians 5:20)

Here are some descriptions about prophets:

"And in these days prophets came from Jerusalem to Antioch." (Acts 11:27);

"Now in the church that was at Antioch there were certain prophets and teachers: Barnabas, Simeon who was called Niger, Lucius of Cyrene, Manaen who had been brought up with Herod the tetrarch, and Saul." (Acts 13:1);

"Now Judas and Silas, themselves being prophets also, exhorted and strengthened the brethren with many words."(Acts 15:32);

"Now this man had four virgin daughters who prophesied." (Acts 21:9);

"And as we stayed many days, a certain prophet named Agabus came down from Judea."(Acts 21:10)

Descriptions about what was prophesied are:

"Then one of them, named Agabus, stood up and showed by the Spirit that there was going to be a great famine throughout all the world, which also happened in the days of Claudius Caesar." (Acts 11:28);

"This charge I commit to you, son Timothy, according to the prophecies previously made concerning you, that by them you may wage the good warfare,"(1 Timothy 1:18) ;

"Do not neglect the gift that is in you, which was given to you by prophecy with the laying on of the hands of the eldership."(1 Timothy 4:14)

Also described are: Precautions to be taken against the activities of false prophets and examples of false prophets in the First Epistle of John, the Gospel of Matthew, the Gospel of Mark and the Acts of the Apostles; the relationship between churches and prophets in the Epistle to the Ephesians and the First Epistle to the Corinthians; supervision of prophecy and some warnings about its use in the First Epistle to the Corinthians; functions of prophets in the end times in the Book of Revelation.

The above examples explain well the importance of prophecy in the work of the Early Church. This of course holds true today. The Lord is willing to work extensively in churches today just as He did in the Early Church. We should not make light of prophecy; prophecy brings forth much good fruit.

The Cross prophets must bear

It is true, however, that various difficulties come to us once we involve ourselves in prophecy. Just as those who carry out God's work cannot avoid taking up the cross, prophets and churches who work in the prophetic will have to take up their crosses.

During a ten-year period after 1975, the excitement that I felt when I first experienced the works of God through prophecy gradually faded away and I began to feel cool toward prophecy. When I met people who were pursuing prophecy or prophesying, I felt they were going to extremes or being sidetracked. The word prophecy made me feel that way even though the people, with a few exceptions, were not going to extremes or being sidetracked.

But one day my attitude toward prophecy was drastically changed when a lady member of our church came and asked me: "Prophecy has been given to me in the Worship Service. May I speak it?" At first, I felt perplexed because I knew what the reaction of people would be. However, the Lord wanted us to use prophecy. As a matter of fact, we were misunderstood by others when we started to use prophecy. However, it was quite a minor thing, compared to the glory of God that we had seen through our use of prophecy. When we start to use prophecy, we will have to bear our cross. We have to brace ourselves for it. We might be misunderstood by our close friends, be blamed by others or suffer heartfelt pain. However, we should never stop using prophecy because we will reap a big reward from it. We should do as 1 Thessalonians 5:18 says, "In everything give thanks; for this is the will of God in Christ Jesus for you." We should thank God for everything because it will equip us for His service, and the Spirit of glory will rest upon us as 1 Peter 4:14 says, "If you are reproached for the name of Christ, blessed are you, for the Spirit of glory and of God rests upon you. On their part He is blasphemed, but on your part He is glorified." When the Spirit of the Lord rests upon us, we will be filled with His Spirit and see His works manifested.

The cross which we have to bear as we do the will of God will bring blessings to us and give us a great victory. We should never abandon prophecy; the Lord greatly reveals His glory through prophecy.

Showing God's glory through sports

The other day, I listened to a testimony by Dwayne Hosey, a professional baseball player from the Yakult Swallows. As of September 18, 1997 Dwayne Hosey has hit 36 homers, and he and Hideki Matsui of the Yomiuri Giants are the two contenders for this season's Home-run King title in the Central League. His testimony revealed that he had lived an extremely hard life. One day, a prophecy was spoken about him and his family through a pastor. The prophecy said that his stepfather would become an evangelist, his mother would help his stepfather's ministry, and that he, Dwayne Hosey, would show the glory of God through sports. This prophecy has now been fulfilled. His stepfather, with a side job, has become an evangelist, his mother helps his ministry, and he, Dwayne Hosey, plays an active part in professional baseball. He said, "At the beginning of this year, everybody said that I wouldn't play well, but God helped me to play successfully. You can see that God has shown His glory in it, can't you?" His achievement is a result of the fulfillment of the prophecy, by which I see God's glory manifested. The Lord works through prophecy. We should use this blessing from God. When we do that, we will see His blessings manifested.

To implement God's plans

As in 1 Corinthians 13 verses 9-10 say: "For we know in part and we prophesy in part. But when that which is perfect has come, then that which is in part will be done away," prophecy accomplishes only a part of God's work. When the perfect comes, prophecy will be done away with. Even though prophecy is a part of God's work, it is important because it is His work; and the Lord will use this gift of prophecy until the perfect comes, i.e., until the Second Coming of Jesus.

God, who implements His plans through power-less people, has His own ways which are different from human ways. Prophecy is one of the important ways for the Lord's work. Through prophecy, we are comforted, prepared and informed of His plans. As for plans and visions, we are often given them which are far beyond our imagination. These visions and plans are fulfilled when we receive them and step forward with them in faith. We should receive what God gives us through prophecy and step forward with it in faith, and then the Lord will manifest His works.

The end-time revival

Several years ago, a prophecy was given to us about Japan. It said that a great revival would take place in Japan, and that Japanese Christians would take the Gospel throughout the world.

Also, one day, a friend of mine, a Romanian prophet gave me this testimony. During World War II, his mother was suffering from incurable breast cancer.

Every effort to cure it failed. At that time, an evangelist with a healing ministry came to the town. His family asked the evangelist to come to his house and pray for his mother's healing. Miraculous healing happened. He saw a new breast appear from under the cancer-affected breast. People who witnessed this miracle were stunned by it, and they were saved, bringing about a small revival. During that revival, some prophecies were spoken about Japan. The first prophecy said that Japan would lose the war; the second said that Japan would miraculously come back and become top in the world economy; and the third said that the end-time revival would start from Japan. As prophesied, Japan lost the war and came out top economically. Therefore, he said, "The prophecy that said that the revival would take place from Japan will also be fulfilled."

A revival will take place in Japan. I am not sure if the end-time revival will start from Japan as prophesied at the lonely village in Romania, but it is certain that a revival will take place in Japan. Many large churches of one thousand, ten thousand and one hundred thousand members will appear in Japan as well. Also, many Japanese missionaries will be sent out to the world with the Gospel just as many missionaries from abroad came to preach the Gospel in Japan. During these times of revival, the Lord will greatly use prophecy and the other spiritual gifts. Various signs of revival have begun to appear in Japan already; the time of God is drawing near.

The Lord says, "Do not despise prophecies." (1 Thessalonians 5:20) Should we not meditate on the meaning of this Scripture once more? God does not speak words unless he has something to say. We must not change His words to suit our thinking, which will cause the flow of God's grace to block.

We should not have unreasonable expectations of prophecy. However, we should really avoid holding back the work of prophecy, not to be involved in it. The time of the Second Coming and that of the great harvest are drawing near. We must move forward, led by the Lord, with all His provisions. Prophecy is one of those provisions.

Final Chapter

❧

In a manner of speaking, the function of prophecy has been forgotten in the Christian world. However, it has a special role for the end times. It is also very helpful in building us up, encouraging us, and fulfilling God's plans. The Lord has placed this gift of prophecy within easy reach of Christians. If we step out for it by faith, the Lord will greatly manifest His works through prophecy. We should seek this gift and use it as the Bible says. We should never make light of any of the Lord's work of blessing even if it is only a part. For, through prophecy, the Lord has the plan to be fulfilled and the work to be done.

In July 1998, we sent an outreach team to Spain. The Lord had told us through prophecy to wage spiritual warfare against a spirit of Mary which was regarded as the guardian deity of Spanish speaking countries in South America. The purpose of the spiritual warfare was to open the way for missions in those countries. We tested the prophecy and were convinced that it was of God. We then went to Spain and waged spiritual warfare in two places dedicated to Mary and we also ministered at a church in Madrid. At that time, I had a sense of victory through the spiritual warfare, but the way to the Spanish speaking countries in South America remained closed.

At the end of February 1999, we sent a team to Peru, a Spanish speaking country in South America. The Lord had told us that He would provide us with relationships in Peru and He also instructed us to wage spiritual warfare there. Then an amazing thing happened. The Lord instructed one of our pastors to contact a Brazilian pastor in Japan; the Brazilian pastor gave him the e-mail address of one of his Spanish friends living in Spain, who then gave him the e-mail address of the pastor of a church in Peru. The pastor of our church had never met that Peruvian pastor, but he sent an e-mail to him asking for an opportunity to minister. Usually, very few churches would accept an offer from an unknown person. However, we received a reply from the Peruvian pastor saying that we would be very welcome. It was a great surprise to us. After our spiritual warfare in Spain, the Lord surely opened up a mission work in a Spanish speaking country in South America. We were given opportunities to minister at six meetings, including worship services at a church in Lima, the capital of Peru, and in Cuzco, the capital of the Inca Empire. We learned that the church we ministered at had eight more churches throughout Peru, and that our e-mail letter went to the head pastor of these churches.

When I talked to that pastor, I was amazed to find out God's plan. Actually, he said that he had come to Japan a few years before. During that stay in Japan, he was shown his calling to Peruvians, Brazilians and other South Americans living in Japan. God then told him to move to Japan with his family. However, he had no connection with any Japanese, and it seemed impossible for him and his family to obtain permanent visas to Japan. The way to Japan had not been opened to him no matter how much he had prayed. Just when he was feeling depressed and discouraged, wondering what would happen to his calling, he received an unexpected e-mail from an unknown church in Japan with a request for an opportunity to minister. He said that he had hardly told anyone his e-mail address at that time. He was very impressed, saying, "I don't know how unknown Japanese got to know my e-mail address."

It was God who did this. It is so marvelous that the pastor was convinced again about his calling to Japan because we Japanese strangers had visited him. After having discussions with us, it was decided that he would leave his work to another person in Peru and move to Japan with his family the following year. He will obtain a visa to Japan as one of our missionaries, and it is planned that he will start a pastoral ministry in Gunma Prefecture. Also his coming to Japan as our missionary provides us with solid foundation for our work in Peru, because he is the leader of eight churches in that country. He said that he would help us with everything we needed, including obtaining visas when we send our missionaries to Peru.

In July 1998 when the Lord told us to wage spiritual warfare to open up mission work in Spanish speaking countries in South America, we just obeyed Him without knowing how it would develop. However, in less than a year, He opened an amazing plan of God. Prophecy has played a major role in realizing this plan. Without prophecy, our relationship with the church in Peru would not have been established and this plan of His would not have been accomplished. We should never make light of the work of prophecy; there are some plans that cannot be accomplished without it. When we run up against a wall in our life or in the walk of the church, there is a way to break through the wall. It is God's guidance, and prophecy will be greatly used in understanding His guidance as well.

A few years ago, a female member in our church introduced me to a young man whom she was considering marrying. He was a Japanese Brazilian and had dedicated his life to work at a prayer house in the Kanto District. Since he was once an amateur wrestler, he ministered there doing heavy work such as digging holes, driving cars, etc. When I prayed for him, the Lord said to him through prophecy, "Your calling is different from what you do now. Your calling is spiritual, such as preaching and counseling." While prophesying I wondered if it was true, because he was not very good at speaking Japanese and also he was a man of few words. Later, various things were shown about him: he would be used as an interpreter; he would be used to establish relationships, and so on. In these situations he began to obey the voice of God. He later left the prayer house and came to our church because the prayer house held to a teaching on the Trinity that was far deviated from the truth. He is now one of the pastors in our church. He preaches many times a week; his Japanese has improved so much that nobody can believe he was once a man of few words. He is also used as an interpreter in Portuguese and Spanish; he has worked as an interpreter for our ministry in Brazil, Spain and Peru, as well as in Brazilian churches in Japan. He has interpreted messages in large meetings in those nations. In one of those meetings there were more than two thousand people.

Also, the Lord has continued establishing relationships through him as prophesied. They include churches in Brazil, Spain and Peru, well-known soccer players from Brazil, Brazilian pastors in Japan and a TV-evangelist in Brazil. We have made so many relationships through him. What God said about him has been fulfilled.

The other day, when we passed the prayer house he once belonged to, he said with a smile that he would still have been digging holes if he had not obeyed the Lord. The Lord told him about the new way, and he heard and obeyed the Lord. Then God's plan for him began to be fulfilled.

These are the things the Lord is going to do through prophecy. We should not neglect gifts from the Lord. If we make light of them, including the gift of prophecy, we will miss out on some of the Lord's blessings. When we seek and use them as the Lord tells us, we will see His abundant blessing being given to us. We should never disregard the gift of prophecy that the Lord has provided for us. We must defeat the enemy with this powerful weapon and implement the Lord's plans. The time has already come.

About the Author

❧

Paul Akimoto is the senior pastor at The Lord's Cross Christian Center Tokyo Antioch Church. He received the baptism of the Holy Spirit while attending the evangelical theological school in 1973.

He goes on an overseas mission trip on a monthly basis; he has visited 82 countries on the five continents (as of December 2012).

The Lord's Cross Christian Center Tokyo Antioch Church

http://tokyo.antioch.jp/

CPSIA information can be obtained at www.ICGtesting.com
Printed in the USA
BVOW11s1034240714

360357BV00027B/464/P